PageMaker 7.0

A Quick Reference of More Than
300 PageMaker Tasks, Terms and Tricks

From A to Z

D0193394

Marc Campbell

Pagemaker 7.0 From A to Z:
A Quick Reference of More Than 300 PageMaker Tasks, Terms and Tricks

Copyright © 2001 Marc Campbell

Published by
Redmond Technology Press
8581 154th Avenue NE
Redmond, WA 98052
www.redtechpress.com

Library of Congress Catalog Card No: applied for

ISBN 1-931150-50-8

Printed and bound in the United States of America.

9 8 7 6 5 4 3 2 1

Distributed by
Independent Publishers Group
814 N. Franklin St.
Chicago, IL 60610
www.ipgbook.com

Designer: Minh-Tam S. Le
Editor: Paula Thurman

INTRODUCTION

If you flipped through this book before reading the Introduction, you probably noticed that *PageMaker 7.0 From A to Z* is different from other books about PageMaker. For one thing, this book arranges its information alphabetically. When you need to define a term or perform a task in PageMaker, you know exactly where to look. But when read from start to finish, this handy quick reference undergoes a transformation. It becomes a kind of storybook that uses PageMaker concepts to help you learn your ABCs. Before you dive in, though, you may find it helpful to understand what this book assumes about your computer skills, what you should know about the PageMaker program, what you need to know about commercial printing, and what editorial conventions this book uses. This short Introduction provides this information.

What You Should Know About Your Platform

You don't need to be a computer expert to use PageMaker, and that means you don't need to be a computer expert to use this book. To get the most out of PageMaker, you should be comfortable working with your computer and your Windows or Macintosh operating system. If you need a crash course in Windows or Mac OS, see the documentation that came with your computer, get a friend to step you through the basics, or acquire a book on your operating system.

NOTE   *PageMaker 7.0 comes in two versions—one for Windows and one for Mac OS—but this book covers both versions. The two PageMakers are very, very similar. In most cases, the same definition for a term or procedure for a task applies to both. In the few cases where the procedures vary, this book gives instructions for Windows users followed by instructions for Mac OS users.*

What You Should Know About PageMaker

PageMaker 7.0 is a powerful tool for desktop publishing. You don't need to know anything more than that to use this book. However, you might find it helpful to play with the program for an hour or two before getting down to more serious business. That way, you become familiar with the user interface and PageMaker's responses to your commands. Just do something goofy, and don't worry about crashing your computer. PageMaker can handle a little fun. If you open a dialog box that you don't want, just click the Cancel button. If you don't know where to begin, refer to the diagram in Figure 1.

The *title bar* gives the name of the current publication.

The *menu bar* lists commands and options for your publication.

The *Toolbar*, available to Windows users, provides clickable icons for many common commands.

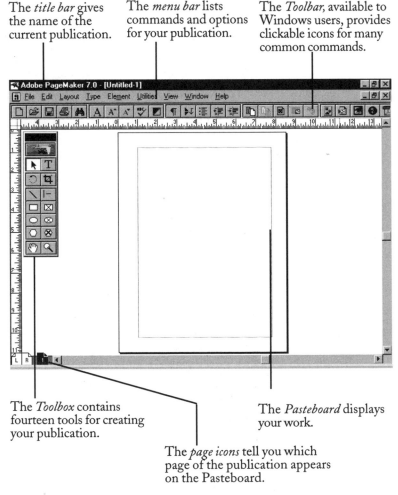

The *Toolbox* contains fourteen tools for creating your publication.

The *Pasteboard* displays your work.

The *page icons* tell you which page of the publication appears on the Pasteboard.

Figure 1   Meet the PageMaker user interface.

The other floating boxes that you see on screen are the palettes (see Figure 2). These provide additional commands and options for your publication. The beauty of the palettes is that you can open them when you need them and close them when you don't. Click the little X icons on the palettes to close them, and, to open them again, use the Show commands in the Window menu.

Figure 2   Palettes like these help you to define and organize different aspects of your publication.

What You Should Know About Commercial Printing

Not everyone prints PageMaker publications on a desktop printer. In fact, many people use PageMaker to create publications specifically for the commercial printing press. PageMaker's high-end printing features help to set this software apart from other desktop publishing applications. While compositors and publishing professionals rejoice, because PageMaker speaks their language, the marketing associate who wants to create a color-photo-copied flyer for a trade show may feel a bit daunted by the sheer number of choices in doing what seems like a simple thing, such as adding the color red.

This book goes into detail about the commercial-printing capabilities of PageMaker. If you plan to send your work to a service provider, you can use this book to get up to speed on technical terms like spot and process color, bleed, trapping, knockout, and overprinting. Make no mistake: You still want to discuss your job thoroughly with your commercial printer, but this book can help you to ask the right questions, and it can show you exactly how to prepare your work for the press.

If you plan to print to your desktop printer or the marketing department's color copier, you can ignore the extra detail in this book, because it simply doesn't apply. It doesn't matter if you choose a process-color red or a spot-color red. It doesn't matter if you use knockouts or overprints. Whether you set up your publication correctly or not-so-correctly for the press, you achieve identical results on an in-house printer, so don't sweat the finer points.

What You Should Know About This Book

You already know the most important feature of this book—that it organizes its task descriptions and term definitions alphabetically. Here are the other conventions.

- When this book refers to some box or button label, the label appears in initial-capital style. For instance, when PageMaker's Paragraph Specifications dialog box offers the option "Keep lines together," it appears as Keep Lines Together in this book. The initial capital letters signal you to the fact that Keep Lines Together is an item in the dialog box.

- This book contains pictures from the Windows version of PageMaker 7.0. If you use PageMaker 7.0 for Mac OS, you may be thrown off a little at first, because windows in Mac OS have a different style and aesthetic sense than those in Windows. However, if you look closely at the labels and buttons in the windows on screen, they should match up with the pictures in the book.

- This book's pictures of windows and dialog boxes may look a bit condensed because they use a low screen setting. This makes the text easier to read. You probably use a higher resolution display, which means that PageMaker fits more comfortably in its window. If you want your display to match the pictures in this book more closely, switch your screen setting to 640 by 480 pixels.

And that, as they say, is that. Time to make some pages. Relax, get comfortable with the software, and don't forget to have fun. If you get stuck, don't fret. This book will help you.

May thy ink never smeareth.

Marc Campbell

marc@taotezing.com

Philadelphia, Pennsylvania, August 2001

PAGEMAKER 7.0 FROM A TO Z

Acrobat Distiller

Acrobat Distiller 5.0 is a standalone application that changes PostScript files to PDF files (see Figure A-1). While Acrobat Distiller isn't required to run PageMaker, it's a crucial component of the Export To PDF feature. You should install Acrobat Distiller from the PageMaker 7.0 Application CD if you plan to distribute your publications electronically.

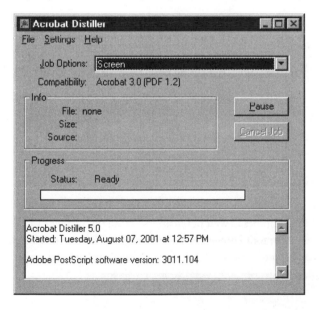

Figure A-1   Acrobat Distiller changes PostScript files to PDF files.

Acrobat Reader

The PageMaker 7.0 Application CD includes Adobe Acrobat Reader 5.0, which opens and reads PDF files (see Figure A-2). PageMaker allows you to export your publications in PDF format, but you need this software to view them. If you don't already have Acrobat Reader on your computer, you should install it from the CD. Your audience can download the program free of charge from the Adobe Web site at *http://www.adobe.com*.

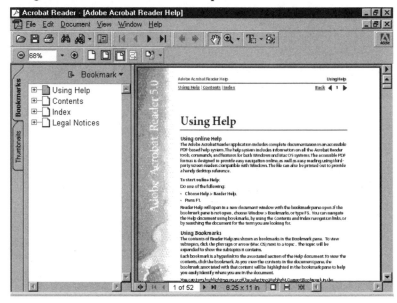

Figure A-2   Acrobat Reader opens PDF files.

Adobe Gallery Effects

Adobe Gallery Effects are Photoshop-style filters that you can use to enhance TIFF graphics in your publication. To use them, select a TIFF graphic with the Pointer tool, choose Element→Image→Photoshop Effects, and pick from the list in the Photoshop Effects dialog box (see Figure A-3).

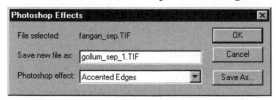

Figure A-3   The Photoshop Effects dialog box lets you apply Adobe Gallery Effects to TIFF images.

PageMaker saves the filtered image with a slightly different filename, puts it in the same location as the original, and links to it. If you want to save the filtered image to a different location, click the Save As button. You can also overwrite the original image with the filtered version by supplying the identical filename, but why would you want to do that? *Always* keep a version of the original image! You can't undo the filter after you apply it, so the only way to correct a mistake is to replace the modified version with the original.

Adobe Table; see Tables

Aligning and Distributing Objects

The Align command arranges two or more objects in relation to each other. To use this command, follow these steps:

1. Grab the Pointer tool from the Toolbox and select the objects you want to align. You must select at least two objects.

2. Choose Element→Align Objects. The Align Objects dialog box appears (see Figure A-4).

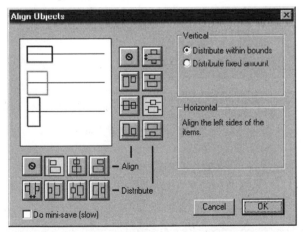

Figure A-4   Use the Align command to arrange objects in relation to each other.

3. The top row of buttons under the white box sets horizontal alignment. From left to right, the choices are None, Align Left, Align Center, and Align Right. Select an option. The colored rectangles inside the box change position to give you an example of the effect.

4. The first row of buttons to the right of the box sets vertical alignment. From top to bottom, the choices are None, Align Top, Align Center, and Align Bottom.

5. If you want to distribute the objects horizontally, select an option from the second row of buttons under the white box. Pick the Distribute Within Bounds option to reposition the objects within the space they currently occupy on the page. Pick the Distribute Fixed Amount option to reposition the objects within an area that you define, be it larger or smaller than the current space. If you specify a negative number for the fixed amount, the objects overlap.

6. If you want to distribute the objects vertically, select an option from the second row of buttons to the right of the box. Choose Distribute Within Bounds or Distribute Fixed Amount.

7. Check the Do Mini-Save option if you want to save your work before aligning. You can't undo an align action, so use the mini-save, especially if you're new to PageMaker.

8. Click OK.

9. Check your publication. If you don't like the results and you opted for the mini-save, hold down Shift and choose File→Revert.

TIP   *When you begin to design a publication, don't worry about positioning the elements precisely. Wait to use the Align command until you are satisfied with the layout.*

Aligning Text; see Text

Anchor

An anchor is a hyperlink target within your publication. Use the Hyperlinks palette to define anchors.

Arranging Objects

Normally, objects stack on the Pasteboard in the order that you added them to your publication. If you want to position two or more objects in the same space, you may need to rearrange the stacking order so that the correct object sits on top. To do so, grab the Pointer tool from the Toolbox and select one of the objects. Then, use one of the following commands:

- Choose Element→Arrange→Bring To Front to move the object to the top of the stacking order.

- Choose Element→Arrange→Bring Forward to move the object one position forward in the stacking order.

- Choose Element→Arrange→Send Backward to move the object one position backward in the stacking order.

- Choose Element→Arrange→Send To Back to move the object to the bottom of the stacking order.

Autoflow

The Autoflow option allows you to place an entire story in threaded text blocks. This prevents you from having to thread the story manually. To place a story with Autoflow, follow these steps:

1. Select Layout from the menu bar and place a check mark next to the Autoflow option at the bottom of the list (see Figure A-5).

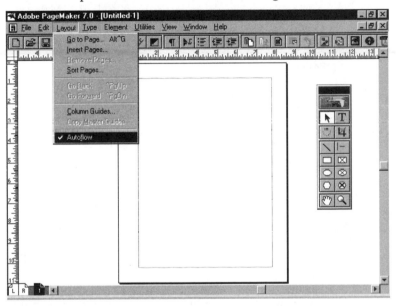

Figure A-5   Check the Autoflow option in the Layout menu to turn on Autoflow.

2. Choose File→Place. Windows users can click the Place button on the Toolbar.

3. Locate the text file you want to place and double-click the icon.

4. The mouse pointer changes into the automatic text flow icon. Note that holding down Ctrl (Windows) or Command (Mac OS) changes the mouse pointer to the manual text flow icon. Use this option if you want to flow the first few columns or pages of the story manually.

5. Position the mouse pointer where you want the story to begin, and click. PageMaker fills the rest of the column or page with text and creates enough new pages to finish the story.

NOTE   *Autoflow creates new pages based on the current master page design. If you place a story on a page with two columns, but the current master page has only one column, Autoflow adds one-column pages to your publication.*

Baseline

The baseline of a line of type is like the rule on a sheet of notebook paper. Most characters sit on the baseline. Characters like the lowercase *p* and *q* have descenders, which dip below the baseline. In PageMaker, reference the baseline to set the leading of a line of type or shift the vertical position of a character in relation to the rest of the line.

SEE ALSO *Character Baseline*

Baseline Guides

Baseline guides are horizontal ruler guides that the Grid Manager plug-in sets in relation to a leading value. Use baseline guides to align paragraphs precisely on the page.

SEE ALSO *Layout Grids, Rulers*

Bitmap Fonts

Bitmap fonts are character sets made up of pixels, or tiny rectangles. Unlike outline fonts, bitmaps often lose crispness when you scale them. If you have bitmap fonts on your computer, you can use them in your PageMaker publication. However, when at all possible, choose outline fonts like TrueType or PostScript Level 1 instead.

Bitmap Graphics

Bitmap or raster graphics are images made from pixels, which are very small, colored rectangles. Bitmaps are resolution-dependent, meaning that they display at a set number of pixels per inch. Because of this, stretching or resizing a bitmap image often causes a loss of image quality: The rectangular shape of the individual pixels becomes noticeable, giving the image a blocky or jagged appearance (see Figure B-1).

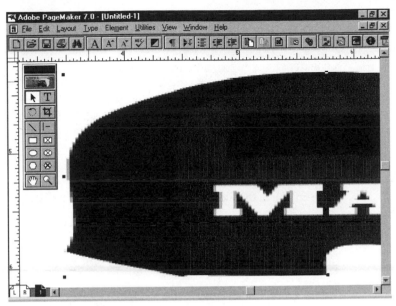

Figure B-1   Somebody stretched this bitmap graphic too much. Notice the loss of crispness along the curve.

PageMaker allows you to place and manipulate several different kinds of bitmap graphics, including JPEG, GIF, TIFF, and BMP. PageMaker also provides a magic stretch feature that helps to reduce loss of image quality.

SEE ALSO *Graphics*

Bleed

In printing, bleed refers to ink that prints outside the boundaries of the page. Commercial printers rely on bleed to put colored elements exactly on the edge of the paper. This process invariably costs extra, because the printer uses slightly larger paper and trims it to size afterwards. In addition, many desktop printers won't print outside set margins, much less at full bleed. If you plan to distribute your publication in printed form, keep to the margins. If you must bleed, bleed sparingly!

PageMaker's default image bleed is one-eighth of an inch. You can extend the bleed to a full inch when saving your publication as a PostScript file.

Book Lists

A book list is a collection of PageMaker files that acts in some respects like a single publication. You can generate a common index and table of contents for the book list, and you can print the entire collection in a single stroke. But because each item is a separate publication, you can work on the components independently and save system resources. A single publication may belong to several different book lists, but it can contain only one book list at a time.

Creating a Book List

To create a book list, follow these steps:

1. Open one of the files that you want to include in the book list.

2. Choose Utilities→Book. The Book Publication List dialog box appears (see Figure B-2).

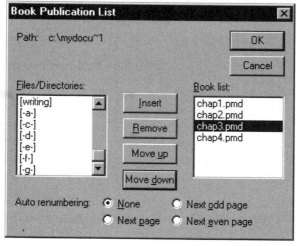

Figure B-2   Set up a book list with the Book Publication List dialog box.

3. Navigate the Files/Directories list on the left until you find a publication that you want to include. Double-click the filename, or highlight it and click Insert. The publication appears in the book list on the right. Repeat this step for every publication that you want to add. If you add a publication by mistake, just highlight the filename in the book list and click Remove.

4. Revise the order of the items in the book list by highlighting the filename on the right and clicking Move Up or Move Down. PageMaker paginates your book from the top of the list to the bottom, so make sure the running order is correct.

5. Choose an option for renumbering the pages. The None option preserves the page numbering of each publication. The Next Page option renumbers the pages consecutively. The Next Odd Page option renumbers the pages consecutively, but each publication on the list begins with an odd number. If necessary, PageMaker inserts a blank page between publications to force the numbering to fall on an odd page. The Next Even Page option works like the previous one, only each publication begins with an even number.

6. Click OK.

Copying a Book List

If you want to create an index and table of contents for the collection as a whole, you need to copy the book list to every publication. To copy a book list, follow these steps:

1. Open the publication that contains the book list.

2. Hold down Ctrl (Windows) or Command (Mac OS) and select Utilities→Book.

This procedure creates an identical—but separate—book list in each publication. If you update one of these book lists in the future, be sure to copy the updated version to all the other publications in the list.

Deleting a Book List

To delete a book list, follow these steps:

1. Open the publication that contains the book list.

2. Choose Utilities→Book.

3. Highlight the first filename in the book list. Click Remove.

4. Continue clicking Remove until the book list is empty.

5. Click OK.

This procedure deletes the book list in a single publication only. If you copied the book list to other publications, you should repeat these steps for each publication.

Editing a Book List

To edit a book list, open the publication that contains the book list and choose Utilities→Book. Remember to copy the edited book list to all the other publications in the collection if you want to compile a general index or table of contents.

Printing All the Publications in a Book List

To print the entire collection of publications, follow these steps:

1. Open the publication that contains the book list.

2. Choose File→Print. Windows users can click the Print button on the Toolbar. The Print Document dialog box appears.

3. Select your printer from the Printer list.

4. Find the Book options in the lower left corner of the dialog box. Click the check box to select the Print All Publications In Book option.

5. If you chose a PostScript printer from the list in Step 3, you may print using the paper settings of each individual publication. Click the check box to select this option. If you chose a non-PostScript printer in Step 3, this option is unavailable.

6. Review the other print settings and modify them as needed.

7. Click Print.

Booked Publications, Booklets; see Books and Pamphlets

Books and Pamphlets

Books and pamphlets differ from typical PageMaker publications in that the pages are impositions: That is, multiple pages appear on a single sheet of paper. When you fold and bind the paper, the pages must appear sequentially. PageMaker's Build Booklet plug-in arranges your publication pages so that they print correctly as impositions (see Figure B-3). To open the Build Booklet plug-in, select Utilities→Plug-Ins→Build Booklet.

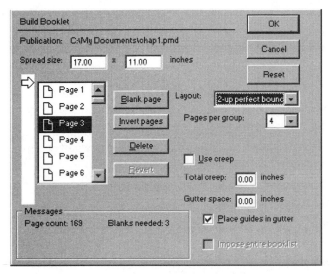

Figure B-3   The Build Booklet plug-in lets you arrange your publication as a book or pamphlet.

Set the following options in the Build Booklet dialog box:

- Specify the spread size, or the size of the paper you plan to use. Remember that multiple pages must appear on a single sheet of paper.

- In the Layout list, choose the type of binding you plan to use. For booklets, select 2-Up Saddle Stitch. This option lets you fold the paper once and fasten the pages at the middle. For books, select 2-Up Perfect Bound to organize the pages into groups, or signatures. You fold and fasten the individual signatures, and then you put the signatures in sequential order and fasten the spine. If you choose this option, set the number of pages per signature in the Pages Per Group list. For pamphlets, select one of the Consecutive options, depending on how many pages or panels should appear on each side of the paper.

- Lengthy booklets or signatures may acquire creep, especially if you print to a heavy paper stock. You can compensate for this by checking the Use Creep option and specifying a value in the Total Creep field.

- To add extra gutter between the pages, type a value in the Gutter Space field.

- To put a ruler guide in the gutter, check the Place Guides In Gutter option.

11

- If your publication contains a book list, check the Impose Entire Booklist option.

You may also use the following commands:

- Under Messages, PageMaker tells you how many blank pages you need to add to your publication to fill out the book. To insert a blank page, choose an insertion point with the arrow icon on the left of the dialog box and click the Blank Page button.

- If you don't want to add blanks, you can always remove unnecessary pages from your publication. To do so, select the page icon and click Delete.

- Click Invert to reverse the running order of the pages, and click Revert to change them back.

When you finish setting up the book or pamphlet, click OK. To restore the defaults, click Reset.

Bulleted Lists; see Lists

Changing Text; see Finding and Changing Text

Character Baseline

PageMaker allows you to change the baseline of a particular character or set of characters in relation to the rest of the type. To modify the baseline of a character, follow these steps:

1. Choose the Text tool from the Toolbox and select the character or characters that you want to modify.

2. Choose Type→Character. The Character Specifications dialog box appears.

3. Click the Options button. The Character Options dialog box appears.

4. Under Baseline Shift, type a value in the Points field and specify whether to shift the baseline up or down by this value. Click OK to close the Character Options dialog box.

5. Click OK in the Character Specifications dialog box.

The character baseline is a character-level attribute that you can set as part of a paragraph style.

SEE ALSO *Paragraph Styles*

12

Character-Level Attributes

Character-level attributes are the characteristics of text that apply to individual characters instead of paragraphs. In other words, a single paragraph can contain pieces of text with different character-level attributes. Examples of character-level attributes include font and leading. To review the attributes of a character, select the character with the Text tool and choose Type→Character (see Figure C-1).

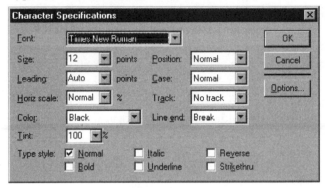

Figure C-1   Review character-level attributes with the Character Specifications dialog box.

SEE ALSO *Paragraph-Level Attributes*

Checking Spelling; see Spelling

Cicero

The cicero is a unit of measurement in typography. One cicero equals 4.51 mm and contains twelve points. The pica is a slightly smaller unit of measure that also contains twelve points.

SEE ALSO *Pica, Point*

Circles; see Ellipses and Circles

CMS

CMS stands for *color management system*. Using a CMS helps to match the colors in your printed publication with the colors you see on screen. Printers and monitors are different kinds of output devices, and they display different gamuts, or ranges of color. A monitor color may not translate well to print, and vice versa. Even if you consider monitors and printers separately, color gamut varies between manufacturer and model. The CMS uses device profiles, or computer files that describe the gamut of your particular hardware, to display color more faithfully between your output devices.

PageMaker for Windows comes with the Kodak Digital Science Color Management System and a large collection of device profiles. PageMaker for Mac OS comes with the Apple ColorSync Color Management System as well as the Kodak CMS and device profiles. Install these components from the PageMaker 7.0 Application CD.

To set up a CMS, follow these steps:

1. Choose File→Preferences→General from the menu.

2. Click CMS Setup to open the Color Management System Preferences dialog box (see Figure C-2).

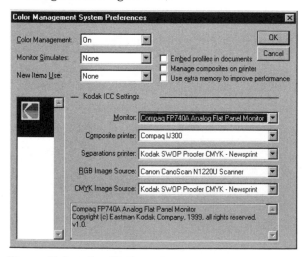

Figure C-2   Set CMS preferences with the Color Management System Preferences dialog box.

3. Select the On option from the Color Management list.

4. The options in the Monitor Simulates list restrict your display to the color gamut of your printer. If you plan to output to a desktop printer, select Composite Printer. If you plan to use a commercial printing service, select Separations Printer. Select None if you don't want to use this feature.

5. Set the New Items Use list to your color management system of choice. This automatically applies your CMS to the objects and colors that you add to your publication.

6. If you plan to save your publication for another computer with a different hardware configuration, select the Embed Profiles In Document option. Adobe recommends that you deselect this option immediately after the save to prevent a drastic drop in performance.

7. If you use a PostScript Level 2 printer or better, selecting Manage Composites On Printer causes the printer itself to handle color management. The Composite Printer device profile becomes unavailable with this option.

8. If you have the RAM to spare, select Use Extra Memory To Improve Performance.

9. Identify device profiles for your hardware. If you don't see the device profile for a particular piece of hardware on your system, use the default setting or contact the manufacturer. Choose the device profile for your monitor from the Monitor list. Choose the device profile for your desktop printer from the Composite Printer list. Choose the device profile for your commercial printer's imaging equipment from the Separations Printer list—you may need to contact your service provider for this information. Choose profiles for your image source devices, such as your scanner or digital camera, from the RGB and CMYK Image Source lists.

10. Click OK.

NOTE   *Some bitmap graphics contain built-in CMS source profiles. PageMaker keeps the embedded CMS source profile for that particular graphic as long as the CMS is available on your computer, no matter what CMS shows in the New Items Use list in Step 5. If the source profile is not available, PageMaker applies the CMS from the New Items Use list as usual. To override a bitmap's embedded CMS source profile as well as the New Items Use list, click the CMS Source button on the Place dialog box during the import procedure and choose the CMS you prefer.*

CMYK

CMYK refers to standard process color printing, which reproduces color by mixing four kinds of ink: cyan, magenta, yellow, and black. PageMaker supports CMYK as well as other color models.

Color

The list of colors in the Color palette determines which colors you can use in your publication (see Figure C-3). If you don't see the Color palette, choose Window→Show Colors.

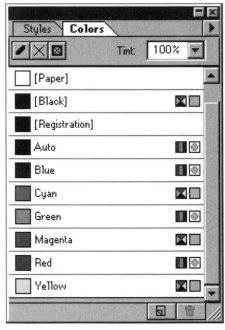

Figure C-3   The Color palette presents the colors of your publication.

When you create a publication from scratch, PageMaker gives you a default set of colors that you can modify to suit your needs. The first four items in the Color palette are common to all PageMaker publications:

- None, or no color at all
- Paper, or the color of the page
- Black, or 100% process black
- Registration, which prints on every plate of a color separation

PageMaker also provides definitions for spot colors blue, green, and red and process colors cyan, magenta, and yellow, but you may edit these colors or add your own as you see fit.

TIP   *Process color is less expensive and fine for most purposes. Stack your palette with process colors if you plan to make a full-color publication. Spot color is generally better and more reliable, but it is also more costly. Reserve spot colors for publications with a limited palette, or use them for select elements that need to print precisely.*

TIP   *If you plan to distribute your publication electronically, always use spot colors, and mix them using the RGB or HLS model. You can convert the spot colors to process colors later if you decide to print your publication commercially.*

Choose additional commands and options from the Color palette menu, which opens when you click the triangle icon in the upper right corner of the palette (see Figure C-4).

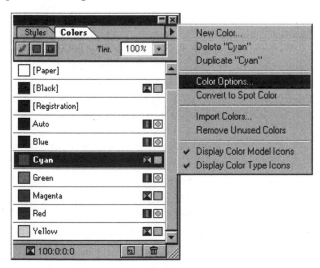

Figure C-4   The Color palette menu opens when you click the tri-angle icon.

Defining Spot or Process Colors

To add a spot or process color to your publication, follow these steps:

1. Click the new-page icon at the bottom of the Color palette. The new-page icon is to the left of the trashcan icon. The Color Options dialog box appears.

2. For a spot color, select the Spot option in the Type list. For a process color, select the Process option.

3. Select RGB, CMYK, or HLS from the Model list. This determines the mixing scheme for the color. If you plan to send your publication to a commercial printer, choose the CMYK model for best color accuracy. Otherwise, choose the model with which you feel most comfortable.

4. Check the Overprint option if you want this color to print on top of other colors instead of knocking out the background in commercial printing.

5. Mix the new color by dragging the sliders or typing numerical values into the fields beside the sliders.

6. Give the new color a name in the Name field.

7. If you want to apply a color management system to this color, click the CMS Source button, choose a CMS from the list, and click OK.

8. Click OK in the Color Options dialog box.

Choosing High-Fidelity Process Colors

High-fidelity process color represents a broader gamut than regular process color. However, not all commercial printers may be able to reproduce high-fidelity colors. Be sure to check with your service provider before you use high-fidelity colors in your publication. To choose a high-fidelity process color, select the Pantone Hexachrome Coated or Pantone Hexachrome Uncoated color library from the Library list in the Color Options dialog box.

Converting Colors

To convert a process color to a spot color or a spot color to a process color, follow these steps:

1. In the Color palette, select the color that you want to convert.

2. Choose Convert To Process Color or Convert To Spot Color from the Color palette menu.

Editing Colors

To edit a color in your publication, follow these steps:

1. In the Color palette, select the color that you want to edit.

2. Choose Color Options from the Color palette menu. The Color Options dialog box appears.

3. Modify the color options to your liking and click OK.

This operation updates all instances of the color in your publication.

Deleting Colors

To remove a color from your publication, follow these steps:

1. In the Color palette, select the color that you want to remove.

2. Click the trashcan icon. PageMaker asks if you want to delete the color. Click OK to proceed.

All instances of the deleted color in your publication change to black.

Replacing Colors

To replace one color with another, follow these steps:

1. In the Color palette, select the color that you want to replace.

2. Choose Color Options from the Color palette menu. The Color Options dialog box appears.

3. Type the name of the replacement color in the Name field. The replacement needs to be a color that already exists in the publication. The name is case-sensitive, so refer back to the Color palette to match the spelling exactly.

4. Click OK. PageMaker asks you to confirm the color replacement. Click OK to update your publication. The old color disappears from the color list, and all instances of the old color in your publication change to the replacement color.

Changing the On-Screen Paper Color

PageMaker assumes that you print to white paper, but this assumption is not always correct. In point of fact, you may print to whatever color paper you choose, no matter what color PageMaker uses to represent the paper on screen. Even still, to get a better feel for your finished publication, you may want to change the on-screen paper color to match the actual paper color. To do so, follow these steps:

1. In the Color palette, select the Paper option.

2. Choose Color Options from the Color palette menu. The Color Options dialog box appears.

3. Pick RGB, CMYK, or HLS from the Model list. This determines how you mix the paper color. Choose the model with which you feel most comfortable.

4. Mix the color by dragging the sliders or typing numerical values into the fields beside the sliders.

5. Click OK in the Color Options dialog box.

NOTE: *You don't have to apply a color management system to the paper color, since this color doesn't print.*

Importing Colors from a PageMaker Publication

You can add the entire set of colors from another PageMaker publication to the color list of the current publication. To do so, follow these steps:

1. Choose Import Colors from the Color palette menu. The Import Colors dialog box appears.

2. In the dialog box, navigate to the PageMaker publication with the colors that you want to import, and double-click the icon.

If you import a different color with the same name as a color in the current publication, PageMaker asks if you want to keep or replace the current color definition.

Importing Colors from an EPS Graphic

EPS graphics contain information about their spot and process colors. PageMaker allows you to import these colors selectively when you place an EPS graphic in your publication. To do so, follow these steps:

1. Choose File→Place from the menu. Windows users can click the Place icon on the Toolbar. The Place dialog box appears.

2. Check the Show Filer Preferences option.

3. Locate the EPS graphic you want to place in your publication and double-click the icon. The EPS Import Filter dialog box appears (see Figure C-5).

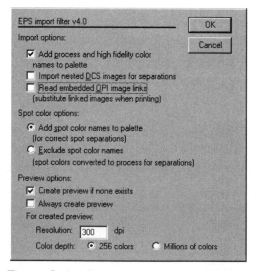

Figure C-5   Import colors from an EPS graphic with the EPS Import Filter dialog box.

4. Check the option for adding process and high-fidelity color names to the Color palette.

5. If your EPS file contains DCS images and you want to import their separation data, check the option for this. Leaving this option unchecked causes PageMaker to import DCS images to a single color plate.

6. Select the option for adding spot-color names to the Color palette. If you want to convert the spot colors to process colors, select the alternate option. Doing so generally reduces the print quality of these colors.

7. Click OK.

If you import a color with the same name as a color in the current publication, PageMaker asks you if you want to replace the current color definition with the imported one.

SEE ALSO *CMS, Color Libraries, Coloring Objects, High-Fidelity Color, Knocking Out Color, Overprinting, Process Color, Spot Color, Tints, Trapping*

Color Libraries

PageMaker's built-in color libraries offer standardized spot and process colors from several commercial color-matching systems, including Pantone. Using colors from these libraries increases the color accuracy of your final printed publication, but check that your service provider supports a particular color library before you choose colors from it. To select a color from a color library, follow these steps:

1. Locate the Color palette on the screen. If you don't see it, select Window→Show Color Palette.

2. Click the new-page icon at the bottom of the Color palette. The new-page icon is to the left of the trashcan icon. The Color Options dialog box appears.

3. Check the Overprint option if you want this color to print on top of other colors instead of knocking out the background.

4. Choose a color library from the Libraries list. The Color Picker dialog box appears (see Figure C-6).

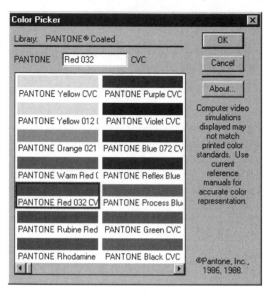

Figure C-6   Use the Color Picker dialog box to select a color from a color library.

5. Drag the slider at the bottom of this dialog box to find the range of colors you want. Then, double-click the color swatch of the precise shade. *Always* confirm your choice with a printed swatch book. If the printed swatch doesn't match the on-screen version, assume that the printed swatch is the more accurate.

6. Click OK in the Color Options dialog box. Resist the temptation to drag the sliders! Doing so changes the definition of the color. Feel free, however, to experiment with tints.

TIP   *PageMaker includes a palette of Web-safe colors in the Online color library. Use this library if you plan to distribute your publication as a Web page.*

Creating a Color Library

PageMaker allows you to save your current color palette as a custom color library for use in other publications. To do so, follow these steps:

1. Choose Utilities→Plug-Ins→Create Color Library. The Create Color Library dialog box appears (see Figure C-7).

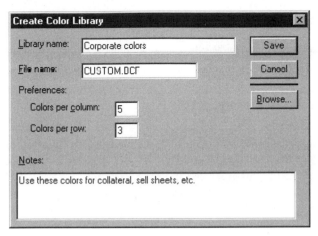

Figure C-7   Define your own color library with the Create Color
Library dialog box.

2. Type a name for the library. This is the name that appears in the Libraries list in the Color Options dialog box.

3. Choose a filename for the library.

4. Set the layout of your color swatches in the Preferences area.

5. Leave instructions or information about your color library in the Notes
   field. The About button in the Color Picker dialog box causes these notes
   to appear.

6. Click Save to save the library in the Color folder, where it needs to be for
   PageMaker to reference it. Click Browse to save the library to some other
   location, such as an external disk drive. However, at some point you must
   move or copy the file to PageMaker's Color folder in order to use the library.

Color Management System; see CMS

Color-Matching Systems; see Color Libraries

Coloring Objects

To apply color to an object, follow these steps:

1. Select the object with the Pointer tool from the Toolbox.

2. Locate the Color palette. If you don't see it, choose Window→Show Colors.

3. Look for three small icons at the top of the Color palette. These determine how to color the object. Click the stroke icon (left) to color the object's stroke. Click the stroke-and-fill icon (middle) to color the entire object. Click the fill icon (right) to color the object's fill.

4. Choose a color from the Color palette. Select a process color for most purposes in a full-color publication. Select a spot color to accentuate a black-and-white publication or ensure that the color of a particular design element reproduces precisely. To make the object transparent, choose None. To make the object invisible, choose Paper. Objects concealed by a paper-colored object won't print. To print the object on every plate of the color separation, choose Registration.

5. You can adjust the tint by pulling down the Tint list. The lower the tint value, the lighter the shade.

Column Guides; see Columns

Columns

Columns control the flow of text on a page. Text-block content repositions itself automatically as you add, remove, and adjust columns.

PageMaker represents columns on screen as column guides, which are dark blue, vertical lines that extend from the top margin to the bottom margin (see Figure C-8). These column guides don't print in your final publication. However, if you find them distracting, you can turn them off with View→Hide Guides.

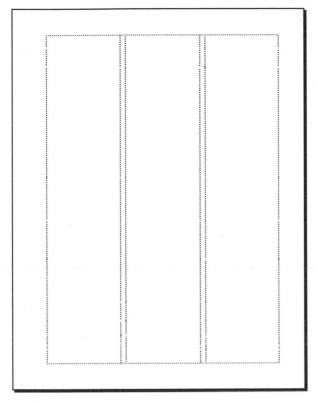

Figure C-8   These are column guides.

TIP   *For better design consistency, apply columns to master pages instead of individual publication pages.*

Creating Columns

To add columns to a page, follow these steps:

1. Turn to the page by clicking on the appropriate page icon at the bottom left.

2. Choose Layout→Column Guides. The Column Guides dialog box appears (see Figure C-9).

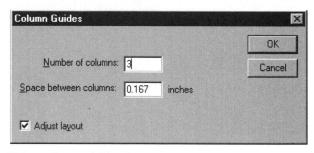

Figure C-9   Add columns to your publication with the Column Guides dialog box.

3. Type the number of columns that you want. The default value is 1. The maximum value is 20.

4. Adjust the gutter, or the space between columns, as you choose. Watch legibility! If your columns are too close, your page becomes difficult to read.

5. Check the Adjust Layout option to reposition and redistribute the elements of the page according to the new column guides. Text in text blocks flows automatically through the new columns. Objects aligned to previously existing columns shift position.

6. Click OK.

Balancing Columns

Balanced columns contain roughly the same number of lines of text. Use balanced columns for a neater, cleaner page design. To balance two or more columns, follow these steps:

1. From the columns on your page, select two or more text blocks. Please note that text frames won't work with this procedure.

2. Choose Utilities→Plug-Ins→Balance Columns. The Balance Columns dialog box appears (see Figure C-10).

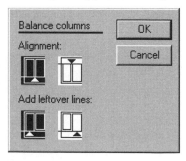

Figure C-10   Balance columns of text in text blocks with the Balance Columns dialog box.

26

3. In the Alignment section, click the icon on the left to align the columns at the bottom. Click the icon on the right to align the columns at the top.

4. In the Add Leftover Lines section, click the icon on the left to add the leftovers to the first column. Click the icon on the right to add the leftovers to the last column.

5. Click OK.

SEE ALSO *Guides, Layout Grids*

Compression

Compression is the process by which computer files, particularly graphics, become smaller. The higher the degree of compression, the smaller the file size, but the more likely that the image quality suffers. To compress a graphics file in PageMaker, follow these steps:

1. Select the graphic with the Pointer tool and choose File→Export→ Graphic. The Export Graphic dialog box appears.

2. Specify a new filename for the compressed image. You may also pick a new format for the compressed image under Save As Type.

3. Click the Settings button in the Export Graphic dialog box.

4. Choose a compression or image-quality setting, and click OK. TIFF and JPEG graphics have four levels of compression each. You can compress GIF images by reducing the color depth, or the total number of colors in the file.

5. Check the Link To New Image option to replace the current graphic with the compressed graphic.

6. Click Save.

If you find that the image quality of the compressed graphic isn't acceptable, replace the compressed graphic with the original and try another compression setting.

TIP   *Your compressed image may look as good as the original, but it will never look better than the original. If you get stuck with a fuzzy source image, consider using an application like Photoshop to improve the image quality before bringing the graphic into PageMaker.*

Constrained-Line Tool

Select the Constrained-Line tool from the Toolbox to draw perfectly horizontal and vertical lines as well as diagonal lines at multiples of 45-degree angles (see Figure C-11).

Figure C-11   Use the Constrained-Line tool to draw lines at multiples of 45-degree angles.

SEE ALSO *Line Tool*

Contents; see Table of Contents

Continued Lines; see Jump Lines

Control Palette

The Control palette is the short, wide floating window in PageMaker (see Figure C-12). This palette allows you to modify the properties of the object in your publication without searching the various PageMaker menus for the same commands. The features of the Control palette change depending upon what you select and what tool you use to select it. For instance, if you select a text object with the Pointer tool, the Control palette lets you change the characteristics of the object, such as its size and orientation. But if you select the text inside the object with the Text tool, the Control palette reconfigures itself to give you full control over the font, point size, leading, and so on.

Figure C-12 The Control palette does just about everything that the menu commands do. This palette changes depending upon the object that you select, but the first icon on the left is always the Apply button.

Modifying an Object with the Control Palette

To use the Control palette to modify an object, select the object with the Pointer tool and choose a reference point from the Proxy, or the square icon with the black dots toward the left side of the palette. The measurements in the Control palette change relative to the reference point that you pick. Then, type a value into the field that corresponds to the characteristic that you want to change. In many fields, you can mix and match measurement systems, and you can also express changes mathematically. The following table lists sample measurements and their meanings:

MEASUREMENT	MEANING
3 in	Three inches
3i	Three inches
3mm	Three millimeters
3p	Three picas
3p4	Three picas, four points
3c	Three ciceros
3c4	Three ciceros, four cicero-points
3 in + 4p	Add four picas to the current measure of three inches
150.5mm − 2c11	Subtract two ciceros, eleven cicero-points from the current measure of 150.5 millimeters
2i * 5	Multiply the current measure of two inches by five
100c / 1.5	Divide the current measure of 100 ciceros by 1.5

After you specify the measurement, click the Apply button, which is always the first icon on the left of the Control palette.

29

You can also use the nudge buttons, or the arrows to the left of the field, to adjust the measurement in small increments. If you use the nudge buttons, you don't have to click the Apply button.

Modifying Text with the Control Palette

To modify text with the Control palette, select the text with the Text tool. For character-level changes, click the text icon to the right of the Apply button, or, for paragraph-level changes, click the paragraph icon. Then, modify the text just like you do for objects: Type values into the fields, or pull standard values from the drop-down lists. Click the Apply button to set your changes. If you use the nudge buttons, you don't have to click Apply.

Setting Options for the Control Palette

You can change the Control palette's nudge units and increments, and you can specify that objects snap to the closest guide on the layout grid when you nudge them into range. To set these options for the Control palette, choose File→Preferences→General.

SEE ALSO *Palettes, Proxy*

Converting Documents

PageMaker 7.0 allows you to open documents created in Microsoft Publisher, Quark XPress, and earlier versions of PageMaker for both Windows and Mac. (PageMaker 7.0 for Mac OS doesn't open Microsoft Publisher files.) You must first convert these publications to a format that PageMaker can use.

Converting Microsoft Publisher and Quark XPress Documents

The Adobe PageMaker 7.0 Converter For Microsoft Publisher/Quark XPress utility, which comes on the PageMaker 7.0 Application CD, converts documents created in Microsoft Publisher 97 and 2000 and Quark XPress 3.3 through 4.1 to PageMaker format. (The converter utility for Mac OS only converts Quark XPress documents.) To use the converter utility, follow these steps:

1. Launch the PageMaker 7.0 Converter For Microsoft Publisher/Quark XPress utility (see Figure C-13). Windows users can find this program under Start→Programs→Adobe→ PageMaker 7.0.

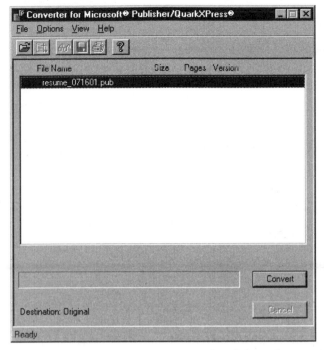

Figure C-13 Convert documents to PageMaker format with the Converter for Microsoft Publisher/Quark XPress utility.

2. Choose File→Select Files.

3. In the Select Files To Convert dialog box, locate and select the Microsoft Publisher document that you want to convert. Windows users can hold down Ctrl to select multiple files at once. Click Select.

4. The filename appears in the main window of the converter utility. Repeat Steps 2 and 3 for as many Publisher documents that you want to convert. If you want to remove a document from the list, select it and choose File→Remove Files.

5. Select the Options menu. If you want to save the converted documents to the same location, keep the Save To Same Folder option checked. You may also click this option to uncheck it and choose a new destination.

6. Choose Options→Conversion Settings to review and change the properties of the converted file. If you're not sure what options to pick, use the default settings.

7. Click the Convert button.

8. Choose View→Show Log for details on the conversion, including any potential problems that the utility found.

Converting Older PageMaker Publications

PageMaker 7.0 converts publications created in PageMaker 4.0 through 6.5 with the Publication Converter plug-in. To use this plug-in, follow these steps:

1. Save and close any open publications.

2. Choose Utilities→Plug-Ins→Publication Converter. The Publication Converter dialog box appears (see Figure C-14).

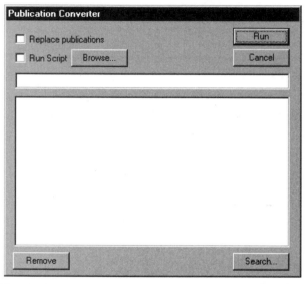

Figure C-14   Use the Publication Converter plug-in to update older PageMaker publications.

3. If you want to create problems for yourself, check the Replace Publications option to overwrite the older files with 7.0 files. Unless your storage space is at a premium, *do not* check this option! *Always* keep copies of your older documents in their original format! You'll be sorry if you don't!

4. Mac OS users can change the extension of the publication by checking the Change Publication Extension option and supplying a new extension. Windows users don't have this option.

5. Click the Search button. The Search For Publications dialog box appears.

6. In the Search For field, supply the filename and extension of the publication that you want to convert. Use the wildcard character (*) to convert all publications of a given type. For instance, to convert all PageMaker 6.5 publications on your system, type *.p65.

7. In the Start From field, type the drive that you want to search.

8. Click OK. The Search For Publications dialog box goes away, and the publications that match your search criteria appear in the main window.

9. To remove a file from the conversion list, select it and click the Remove button. Windows users can hold down Ctrl to select multiple files.

10. Click the Run button to convert all the files in the list.

Converting PageMaker for Mac OS Publications to PageMaker for Windows Format

The Cross-Platform PageMaker Converter transforms Macintosh PageMaker 5.0*x* or 6.0*x* publications to PageMaker 6.0 for Windows format. You can then use the Publication Converter plug-in to change the PM6 file to a PMD for use in PageMaker 7.0. The cross-platform utility does not convert Windows publications to Mac OS format. To run the Cross-Platform PageMaker Converter, follow these steps:

1. Transfer the Mac OS publications to your Windows platform.

2. Launch the Cross-Platform PageMaker Converter (see Figure C-15), which can be found under c:\Program Files\Adobe\PageMaker 7.0\Extras\XplatConv\XPMConv.exe.

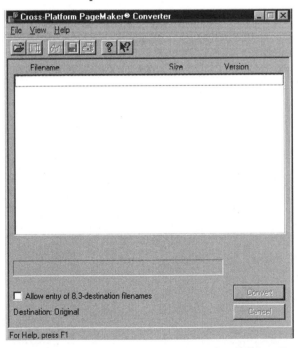

Figure C-15   Use the Cross-Platform PageMaker Converter to change Mac OS publications into Windows publications.

3. Choose File→Select Files.

4. In the Select Files To Convert dialog box, locate and select the publications you want to convert. Hold down Ctrl to select multiple files at once. Click Select.

5. The filenames appear in the main window of the converter utility. If you want to remove a publication from the list, select it and choose File→Remove Files.

6. Select the File menu. If you want to save the converted documents to the same location, keep the Save To Same Folder option checked. You may also click this option to uncheck it and choose a new destination.

7. If you plan to save the converted file across a network, you may need to check the option for entering 8.3-destination filenames, or filenames that contain a maximum of eight characters and a three-character extension. Consult your network administrator.

8. Click the Convert button.

9. Choose View→Show Log for details on the conversion, including any potential problems that the utility found.

TIP   *If you convert Mac files frequently, create a shortcut to XPMConv.exe and store it in the Windows Start Menu under Programs→Adobe.*

Copied Files

By default, when you place an image or text file, PageMaker creates a copy of the file as an object in your publication. You can delete or move the original file without affecting the copy in your publication. However, since copying the file increases the size of your publication, you may choose to link the file to your publication instead.

SEE ALSO *Linked Files*

Copying Objects; see Objects

Creep

Creep occurs in a book or booklet if the edges of the pages don't line up properly when the book closes. The number of sheets per signature and the heaviness of the paper stock contribute to the risk of creep. To determine the amount of creep in your publication, create a dummy signature from the paper stock you plan to use. Bind the pages on one side, trim them so that they line up perfectly on the unbound edge, and measure the difference between the outer sheet of the signature and the inner sheet.

SEE ALSO *Books and Pamphlets*

Cropping Graphics

Crop the images that you place in your publication with the Cropping tool (see Figure C-16).

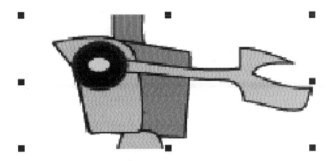

Figure C-16   The Cropping tool changed the visible portion of this graphic.

To crop a graphic, follow these steps:

1. Grab the Pointer tool from the Toolbox and select the graphic that you want to crop.

2. Go back to the Toolbox and select the Cropping tool. The mouse pointer becomes the cropping icon.

3. Change the visible portion of the object by dragging the handles.

4. Release the mouse button, move inside the graphic, and hold down the mouse button again. The cropping icon becomes a hand. Reposition the graphic inside the cropped frame.

5. Repeat Steps 3 and 4 until you like what you see.

NOTE   *Step 3 doesn't work if you use the Cropping tool on frames that you draw with the frame tools.*

Cropping Tool

Select the Cropping tool from the Toolbox to change the visible potion of a graphic or reposition a graphic within a cropped frame (see Figure C-17).

Figure C-17   The Cropping tool lets you change the visible portion of a graphic.

Cutting Objects; see Objects

Dashes

You can type dashes into text objects. Use em dashes in sentences for emphasis—but use them sparingly. Use en dashes to separate ranges of numbers, as in 3–5. The following table shows the keys you should press to type dashes.

DASH	WINDOWS KEYS	MAC OS KEYS
Em	Alt+Shift+-	Option+Shift+-
En	Alt+-	Option+-

Data Merge

PageMaker's Data Merge feature allows you to create multiple publications from data files such as mailing lists. To use Data Merge, you need two components:

- A data source file, which may contain text or paths to images

- A target publication, which receives and places the data in locations that you predefine

These combine to form a brand new, merged publication, which contains multiple copies of the target publication—one copy for each record from the data source file.

The Data Merge palette lets you create a merged publication (see Figure D-1). Display the Data Merge palette by selecting Window→Plug-In Palettes→Data Merge Palette. For additional commands and options, open the Data Merge palette menu by clicking the triangle in the upper right corner of the palette (see Figure D-2).

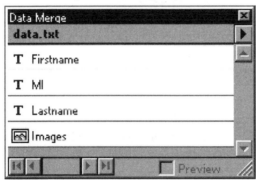

Figure D-1   Use the Data Merge palette to set up a merged publication.

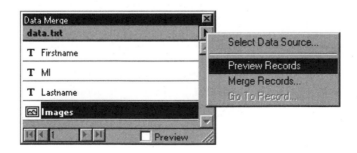

Figure D-2   Open the Data Merge palette menu by clicking the triangle icon.

Creating a Data Source File

To create a data source file from a spreadsheet or database program, follow these steps:

1. Launch your spreadsheet or database program.

2. Load a previously existing data file, or create a new one.

3. Give each column head a unique name; for instance, Firstname, Lastname, MI. These will be the field names that you use in PageMaker when you set up the target publication.

4. Populate the file with data.

5. Save the file in comma-delimited format.

Adobe Table 3.0 comes on the PageMaker 7.0 Application CD. To use Adobe Table to create a data source file, follow these steps:

1. Launch Adobe Table 3.0.

2. Create a new table with File→New.

3. In the first row of the table, provide the names of the columns. These will be the field names that you use in PageMaker when you set up the target publication.

4. Populate the file with data.

5. Choose File→Export→Text, and select Comma-Delimited Text from the Save As Type list on the Export Text dialog box.

You can also use a word processor or text editor to create your data source file. To do so, follow these steps:

1. Launch your word processor or text editor.

2. Create a new document.

3. Type the first line, which gives the names of the columns. These will be the field names that you use in PageMaker when you set up the target publication. Separate each column name with a comma, and don't add space between the comma and the next column name. After the last column name, press Enter.

4. Type one line, again separated by commas, for each record. If a particular entry contains a comma, put the entry in quotes.

5. Save the file in plain text format.

NOTE   *If you want a column in your data source file to contain paths to graphics files, put the "at" symbol (@) in front of the column name, such as @Imagepaths. Then, in the "at" column, indicate the precise path to the graphic for each record. For example, in Windows, a well-formed path might be c:\My Documents\Data Merge graphics\platypus.tif. In Mac OS, the path might be Mac HD:Data Merge Graphics:Playtypus.*

Preparing a Target Publication

To set up the target publication, follow these steps:

1. Open the publication that you want to use as the target, or design a new publication from scratch.

2. Choose the Select Data Source command from the Data Merge palette menu.

3. In the Select Data Source dialog box, navigate to the data source file and double-click the icon (see Figure D-3). The column names from the source file appear in the Data Merge palette—these are the data fields. The icon to the left of the name indicates whether the field is for text or graphics.

Figure D-3   The Select Data Source dialog box lets you import a data source file.

4. To place a text field in your publication, create a new text object, or choose a previously existing one. Use the Text tool from the Toolbox to get a blinking cursor at the insertion point, or highlight the text that you want to replace. Click the text field in the Data Merge palette. The field name appears in the text object between double angle brackets (<<, >>).

5. To place an inline graphics field in your publication, follow the procedure in Step 4, only click the graphics field in the Data Merge palette instead of a text field.

6. To place a floating graphics field in your publication, first deselect all objects in your publication by clicking on white space with the Pointer tool. Then click the graphics field in the Data Merge palette. PageMaker asks if you want to create a floating graphics field. Click OK to proceed. A graphics placeholder appears in your publication. Resize the placeholder to the dimensions of your graphics by dragging the handles with the Pointer tool or, better yet, modifying the values in the Control palette.

7. Repeat Steps 4, 5, and 6 until you place all the data fields you want to merge.

TIP   *PageMaker stretches merged graphics to fit the placeholder. This can distort your images noticeably if they vary too much in size. To avoid this problem, prepare your images to have the same width and height using graphics software such as Photoshop.*

TIP   *To make the placeholder frame the precise size of the graphics you want to merge, use the Control palette. First, check the Preview option on the Data Merge palette, and use the Pointer tool to select the placeholder frame. Then, on the Control-palette Proxy, select one of the corners or the center as the reference point, and set the W and H fields to 100%.*

Previewing the Merged Publication

To preview the merged publication, follow these steps:

1. Open the target publication.

2. Check the Preview option at the bottom of the Data Merge palette.

3. The target publication merges the first record from the data source file.

4. Use the arrow buttons at the bottom of the Data Merge palette to view other records, or open the Data Merge menu and choose Go To Record to jump directly to a particular record.

5. Make changes to the design of your publication accordingly. You can also edit the data source file in its native application, but uncheck the Preview option in PageMaker before you proceed.

Creating the Merged Publication

To create the merged publication, follow these steps:

1. Open the target publication.

2. Choose Utilities→Plug-Ins→Merge Records. The Merge Records dialog box appears (see Figure D-4).

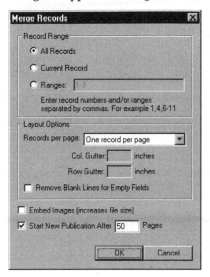

Figure D-4   The Merge Records dialog box sets the options for the merged publication.

3. Select the records that you want to merge under Record Range. Note that the second choice, Current Record, refers to the record number that currently shows between the arrow buttons in the Data Merge palette.

4. Choose the format for the merged publication under Layout Options. If you choose Manual Layout from the Records Per Page list, PageMaker fits as many records on a page as possible. Be sure to set ample gutter space between the columns and rows, or your merged publication may be difficult to read.

5. If your data source file contains optional fields, be sure to check Remove Blank Lines For Empty Fields under Layout Options. This prevents PageMaker from leaving a space in your publication when the optional field does not appear in a particular record.

6. Check the Embed Images option to include copies of merged graphics in the publication. If you leave this option unchecked, PageMaker creates links to the image file on your hard drive. The main disadvantage to linking instead of embedding is that, if you ever move the source files, PageMaker can lose track of them, and your publication displays with broken-image placeholders until you manually fix the links. But, if you have a large data source file and you use many merged graphics, embedding may not be practical, because the file size of the final publication would be enormous.

41

7. Checking the Start New Publication After option creates a brand new merged publication as soon as PageMaker merges the specified number of records. To create a new merged publication for each record, set this value to 1. Otherwise, allow PageMaker to append multiple records into a single file, although too high a value in this field causes unwieldy file sizes. Determine this number based on the size of your data source file and the length and complexity of your target publication. Also keep in mind that the maximum number of pages in a single PageMaker publication is 999.

8. Make changes to the design of your publication accordingly. You can also edit the data source file in its native application, but uncheck the Preview option in PageMaker before you proceed.

9. Click OK. Your merged publications appear in PageMaker for you to print or save.

Deleting Objects; see Objects

Descender

In typography, a descender is the portion of a character that extends below the baseline of a line of type. Letters like the lowercase *a* don't have descenders. Letters like *g, p,* and *q,* do. For the truly curious, the portion of a character that isn't the descender is the body.

If a particular font in your publication has unusually long descenders, such as handwritten or cursive-style lettering, you may need to adjust the leading to improve legibility.

Device Profile

A device profile is a computer file that contains information about the color gamut of your hardware. A color management system (CMS) uses device profiles to ensure consistent, accurate color reproduction for all your input and output devices. The PageMaker 7.0 Application CD comes with device profiles for many popular monitors, printers, scanners, digital cameras, and other pieces of hardware. If you don't find a device profile for your particular component, contact the manufacturer.

Dictionaries; see Language Dictionaries, User Dictionaries

Dictionary Editor; see User Dictionaries

Discretionary Hyphen; see Hyphenation

Documents; see Publications

Double-Sided Publications

A double-sided publication is a PageMaker document that you plan to print using both sides of the paper. You usually organize a double-sided publication into sets of facing pages, or two-page spreads, but, if you don't like to work this way, you don't have to. Under File→Document Setup, if you uncheck the Facing Pages option, PageMaker organizes your double-sided publication into individual pages rather than two-page spreads.

SEE ALSO *Single-Sided Publications*

Drawing Objects; see Ellipses and Circles, Lines, Polygons and Stars, Rectangles and Squares

Drop Caps

A drop cap is a large capital letter at the beginning of a paragraph or chapter. It extends a few lines below the baseline, and the rest of the paragraph wraps around it. To add a drop cap to your publication, follow these steps:

1. Grab the Text tool from the Toolbox, and click anywhere in the paragraph that gets the drop cap.

2. Choose Utilities→Plug-Ins→Drop Cap. The Drop Cap dialog box appears (see Figure D-5).

Figure D-5   The Drop Cap dialog box lets you add a drop cap to a paragraph.

3. In the Size field, supply the number of lines you would like the drop cap to drop.

4. Click the Apply button.

5. Click Close if you are done, or click Prev or Next to move to a new paragraph and apply another drop cap.

To remove a drop cap, click anywhere in its paragraph with the Text tool and open the Drop Cap dialog box. Click the Remove button.

NOTE *You can't change the size of an existing drop cap with the Drop Cap dialog box. Remove the drop cap first, and then apply a new drop cap in the size you want.*

TIP *Editing a drop-capped paragraph is tricky. To edit the word that contains the drop cap, first highlight the drop cap itself with the Text tool and type the new letter. Then highlight the rest of the word and edit it as needed. If your edits cause the line to break in a different place, you may have trouble with formatting. Your best bet is to remove the drop cap, edit the paragraph, and re-apply the plug-in.*

Effects; see Adobe Gallery Effects

Ellipse Tool

Select the Ellipse tool from the Toolbox to draw ellipses and circles (see Figure E-1).

Figure E-1 The Ellipse tool lets you draw ellipses and circles.

Ellipses and Circles

To draw an ellipse or circle, follow these steps:

1. Select the Ellipse tool from the Toolbox. The mouse pointer becomes a crosshairs.

2. Position the crosshairs where you'd like to start drawing, hold down the mouse button, and drag. You can adjust the size and shape of the ellipse as you go. Holding down Shift while you draw changes the ellipse into a circle.

3. Release the mouse button (see Figure E-2).

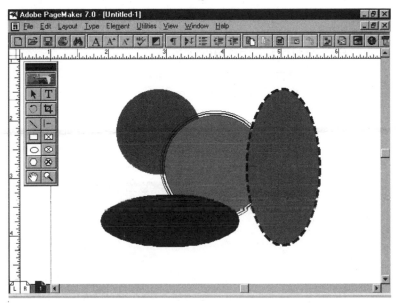

Figure E-2   The Ellipse tool drew these ellipses and circles.

Em Dash; see Dashes

Em Space; see Fixed-Width Spacing

Emulsion Side

The emulsion side of photographic film is the light-sensitive side. Before furnishing your commercial printer with a PostScript file of your publication, be sure to confirm whether the film is emulsion-side up or emulsion-side down. PageMaker's default setting is emulsion-side up, but you can easily change this under File→Print. Choose your PostScript printer driver from the Printers list in the Print Document dialog box, and click the Color button. Check the option for Mirror to print emulsion-side down.

En Dash; see Dashes

En Space; see Fixed-Width Spacing

Exporting Graphics and Text

PageMaker allows you to export your entire publication as a Web page or PDF file, but you can also export individual graphics and pieces of text within your publication.

Exporting Graphics

To export a graphic, follow these steps:

1. Select the Pointer tool from the Toolbox, and select the graphic you want to export.

2. Choose File→Export→Graphic. The Export Graphic dialog box appears (see Figure E-3). In the Graphic Name, Format, Kind, and Source Space fields, review information about the selected graphic.

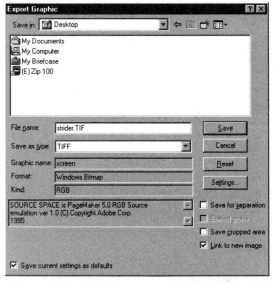

Figure E-3   The Export Graphic dialog box lets you choose the export format and settings for an image.

3. Specify the location and filename for the exported graphic, and choose the format in the Save As Type list.

4. Review and modify options for the exported graphic by clicking the Settings button. The available options depend on the format you select in Step 3.

5. If you use a CMS, you may have options to save the exported graphic for separation or embed the current image's source profile in the exported graphic. Check any that apply.

6. Check the Save Cropped Area option if you want the exported image to resemble the cropped image in your publication. Otherwise, the entire, uncropped image may export.

7. Check the Link To New Image option if you want the exported graphic to replace the current version in your publication.

8. Check the Save Current Settings As Defaults option if you want PageMaker to remember your settings.

9. Click Save.

Exporting Text

To export text, follow these steps:

1. Select the Text tool from the Toolbox.

2. If you want to export an entire story, click anywhere in the story. If you want to export only a portion of the story, highlight the text to export.

3. Choose File→Export→Text. The Export Document dialog box appears (see Figure E-4).

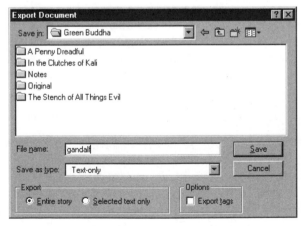

Figure E-4   The Export Document dialog box gives you options for exporting text.

4. Choose a name and location for the exported text file.

5. In the Save As Type list, choose a format for the exported text file.

6. If you highlighted text in Step 2, you have the option of saving the entire story or just the selected text. Pick your preference.

7. Click Save.

Facing Pages

In a book, facing pages are the left and right pages in a two-page spread. When the book is closed, they lay face to face, hence the term. It's customary to allow extra space in the inside margin of a two-page spread to account for binding. To set up your publication for facing pages, choose File→Document Setup and check the options for Double-Sided and Facing Pages.

SEE ALSO *Double-Sided Publications*

Fill

Many PageMaker objects have a fill, or an interior color. Compare this with the stroke, which is the color of the object's contour. To apply a fill to an object, select the object with the Pointer tool and choose Element→Fill And Stroke. Then, pick a style, color, and tint for the fill in the Fill And Stroke dialog box. If you choose Paper for the fill style or color, the fill becomes invisible. Objects underneath the paper-colored fill won't print. If you choose None for the fill style or color, the fill becomes transparent. Objects underneath the transparent fill print as normal. Check the Overprint option if you want the fill to print on top of colors in the background instead of knocking them out. If you want to modify the style of an object's fill quickly, select the object and choose Element→Fill.

NOTE   *Text blocks don't take a fill attribute, but text frames do.*

TIP   *You can apply a fill to a black-and-white graphic. Applying red, for instance, changes the graphic from black and white to red and white, with shades of pink instead of gray.*

Finding and Changing Text

In the Story Editor, the Change command searches your publication's text and, at your discretion, replaces it with different text. To execute the Change command, open the Story Editor with Edit→Edit Story. Then, choose Utilities→Change to open the Change dialog box (see Figure F-1). You can pick Utilities→Find instead, but the Change command does everything that Find does, plus it gives you the ability to replace text.

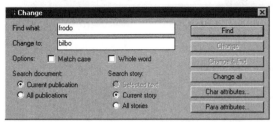

Figure F-1   Search and replace text in the Story Editor with the Change dialog box.

To use the Change dialog box, type the target string, or the text that you want to find, in the Find What field. If you want to change the target string into something else, type the replacement string in the Change To field. If you want to remove the target string, leave the Change To field blank. Then, set the following options:

- Check Match Case if you want to search the text for the exact spelling of the target string. If you select this option, words like *This* and *this* won't register as matches, because the one begins with an uppercase letter. If you don't select this option, the previous example registers a match.

- Check the Whole Word option if you want to find only whole-word matches. For instance, if your target string is *any*, PageMaker finds matches in words like *many* and *Ganymede* unless you check this option.

- Under Search Document, choose if you want to search the current publication or all open publications.

- Under Search Story, choose if you want to search the selected text, the current story, or all stories in the publication.

When you click the Find button, PageMaker scans the text and alerts you of a match. To change the text, click the Change button. To change the text and proceed to the next match, click the Change & Find button. To proceed to the next match without changing anything, click the Find button. Click the Change All button to replace all matches automatically.

You can also search and replace character and paragraph attributes like formatting and styles. To do so, instead of typing a word in the Find What or Change To field, click the Char Attributes (see Figure F-2) or Para Attributes button (see Figure F-3).

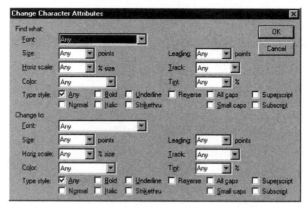

Figure F-2   Find and change character attributes with the Change Character Attributes dialog box.

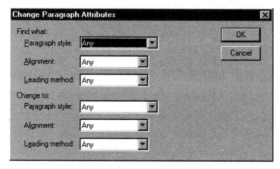

Figure F-3   Find and change paragraph attributes with the Change Paragraph Attributes dialog box.

Specify target and replacement attributes, and click OK. Then, use the Find and Change buttons as before. Please keep in mind that the Story Editor doesn't show most types of text formatting, so it may not appear that your text changes when you find and change attributes. However, if you switch back to layout mode with Edit→Edit Layout, you can see the results.

Fixed-Width Spacing

When you type a spacebar in a text object, PageMaker inserts a variable-width space, meaning that the width of the space character can change in justified text. In some cases, you may want to insert a precise amount of space between words or sentences. PageMaker provides fixed-width spaces for these occasions. As the name implies, fixed-width spaces don't change size in justified text. The width of the space character remains constant.

Choose from three fixed-width spaces: large, medium, and small; or, in typographer's terms, em, en, and thin. The em space derives its name from the lowercase letter *m*, which is traditionally one of the widest letters in a typeface. The en space, after the narrower letter *n*, is one half an em space. The thin space is one-half of an en, or one-quarter of an em. Incidentally, these ems and ens correspond to the widths of em and en dashes.

The following table shows the keys to press to insert fixed-width spaces:

FIXED-WIDTH SPACE	WINDOWS KEYS	MAC OS KEYS
Em space	Ctrl+Shift+M	Command+Shift+M
En space	Ctrl+Shift+N	Command+Shift+N
Thin space	Ctrl+Shift+T	Command+Shift+T

NOTE   *The size of a fixed-width space changes in proportion to the point size of the text, just like a letter character. In other words, a 36-point em space is three times wider than a 12-point em space.*

Floating Graphics; see Independent Graphics

Fonts

Fonts describe the typefaces in your publication. You can use any font on your computer with PageMaker. When you click inside a text object with the Text tool, the Control palette gives you options for setting or changing the font.

Computer fonts generally fall into two categories: bitmap and outline. Bitmap fonts are more problematic in that they don't scale, or change size, very gracefully. If you scale a bitmap font too much, you begin to see the square shape of the pixels that make it up. Outline fonts such as TrueType and PostScript are vector-based, so you can stretch them and scale them as much as you want without sacrificing the sharpness of the text.

Substituting Fonts

The fonts that appear in a publication depend on the computer that created it. If you open a publication from another computer, and your system doesn't have the same fonts that the designer used, PageMaker asks if you want to substitute similar-looking fonts from your system. When this happens, you have the option of choosing your own substitution font, taking PageMaker's recommended choice, or canceling the substitution. Even a close substitution can cause irregularities in design and layout, so obtaining the proper fonts and installing them on your system is the best course of action. You might also remind the designer to include the fonts in the publication the next time around.

Footers; see Running Headers and Footers

Frame Tools

PageMaker provides three tools for drawing frames: the Rectangle Frame tool, the Ellipse Frame tool, and the Polygon Frame tool (see Figure F-4). Select these tools from the Toolbox to add frames to your publication.

Figure F-4   The Rectangle, Ellipse, and Polygon Frame tools let you draw frames.

Frames

Frames in PageMaker are container-type objects for graphics or text. They may be rectangular, elliptical, or polygonal in shape. The advantage to putting a graphic in a frame instead of placing it directly into PageMaker is that you can resize the frame to fit the design of your publication without changing the size or aspect ratio of the graphic inside it. The advantage of putting text in a frame instead of a text block is that the frame can have any conceivable shape in addition to fill and stroke attributes.

When you click a frame with the Pointer tool, windowshade handles appear (see Figure F-5). You find windowshades only on frames and text blocks.

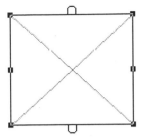

Figure F-5   A frame gives you windowshade handles when you select it.

Drawing a Rectangular Frame

To draw a rectangular frame, follow these steps:

1. Select the Rectangle Frame tool from the Toolbox. The mouse pointer becomes a crosshairs.

2. Position the mouse pointer where you want to start drawing, hold down the mouse button, and drag. Adjust the size and shape of the frame as you go (see Figure F-6). Pressing Shift while you draw changes the rect angle into a perfect square.

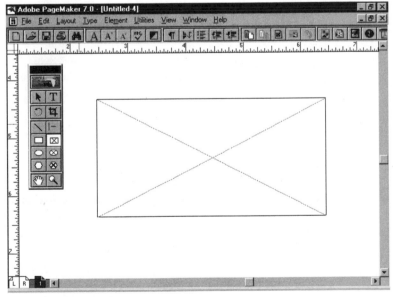

Figure F-6   The Rectangle Frame tool drew this rectangular frame.

3. Release the mouse button.

53

4. To round the corners of the frame, choose Element→Rounded Corners. The Rounded Corners dialog box appears. Select one of the rounding styles and click OK.

Drawing an Elliptical Frame

To draw an elliptical frame, follow these steps:

1. Select the Ellipse Frame tool from the Toolbox. The mouse pointer becomes a crosshairs.

2. Position the mouse pointer where you want to start drawing, hold down the mouse button, and drag. Adjust the size and the shape of the frame as you go. Pressing Shift while you draw changes the ellipse into a perfect circle.

3. Release the mouse button (see Figure F-7).

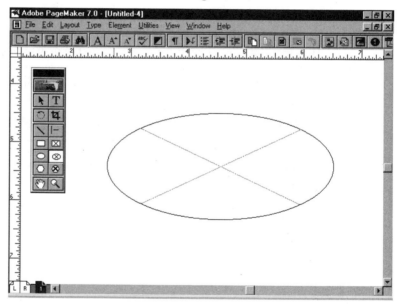

Figure F-7   The Ellipse Frame tool drew this elliptical frame.

Drawing a Polygonal Frame

To draw a simple polygonal frame, follow these steps:

1. Select the Polygon Frame tool from the Toolbox. The mouse pointer becomes a crosshairs.

2. Position the mouse pointer where you want to start drawing, hold down the mouse button, and drag. Adjust the size and the shape of the frame as you go (see Figure F-8). Pressing Shift while you draw constrains the proportions of the polygon.

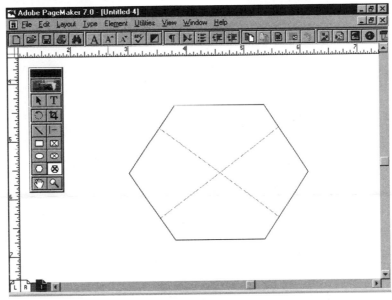

Figure F-8   The Polygon Frame tool drew this simple polygonal frame.

3. Release the mouse button.

4. To change the number of sides of the polygon or transform the polygon into a star, select Element→Polygon Settings.

To draw a complex polygonal frame, follow these steps:

1. Select the Polygon Frame tool from the Toolbox. The mouse pointer becomes a crosshairs.

2. Position the mouse pointer where you want to start drawing, and click and release the mouse button.

3. Move the mouse to draw the first side of the frame. Hold down Shift to constrain the angle to multiples of 45 degrees.

4. Click the mouse button to start a new side, and continue drawing. You can add as many sides to the frame as you like.

5. To finish, join the end point of the last side to the start point of the first. A small square appears at the intersection. Click the mouse button, and the frame closes (see Figure F-9).

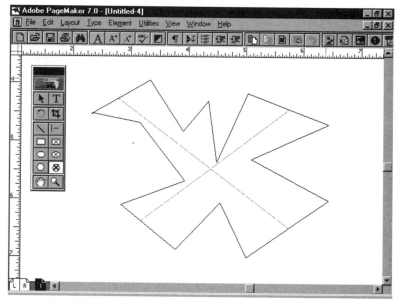

Figure F-9   The Polygon Frame tool drew this complex polygonal frame.

Attaching Content to a Frame

To put content from your publication into a frame, follow these steps:

1. Grab the Pointer tool from the Toolbox.

2. Holding down Shift, select the content you want to attach and the frame to which you want to attach it.

3. Choose Element→Frame→Attach Content.

To place a new text or graphics file into a frame, follow these steps:

1. With the Pointer tool, select the frame into which you want to place the content.

2. Choose File→Place. Windows users can click the Place icon on the Toolbar. The Place dialog box appears.

3. Navigate to the file you want to place, and double-click the icon. The text or graphics file appears in the frame.

Detaching Content from a Frame

To separate a frame and its content, follow these steps:

1. Select the frame with the Pointer tool.

2. Choose Element→Frame→Separate Content. The content becomes an independent object.

TIP   *If you would rather erase the content of the frame entirely, choose Element→Frame→Delete Content in Step 2.*

Positioning Content Within a Frame

To change the position of the content in a frame, follow these steps:

1. Select the frame with the Pointer tool.

2. Choose Element→Frame→Frame Options. The Frame Options dialog box appears (see Figure F-10). The available options depend on the type of content and the shape of the frame. In general, text content has inset options and some positioning, while graphics content has more positioning options but no inset.

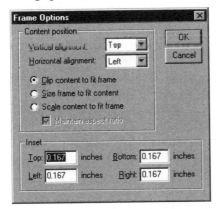

Figure F-10   Set options for positioning frame content in the Frame Options dialog box.

3. Choose vertical and horizontal alignment options, if available.

4. For graphics, choose clipping the content to fit the frame, sizing the frame to fit the content, or scaling the content to fit the frame. When scaling, check Maintain Aspect Ratio to avoid distorting the image. Otherwise, the image stretches to fit precisely in the frame.

5. For text, specify values for the inset, or the amount of space between the frame border and the text area. If you don't want a cushion of space around the text, set these values to 0.

6. Click OK.

TIP   *To reposition a graphic in a frame with a much greater degree of control, use the Cropping tool from the Toolbox.*

Changing an Object into a Frame

You can easily convert objects that you draw with the Rectangle, Ellipse, and Polygon tools into frames. To do so, follow these steps:

1. With the Pointer tool, select the drawn object that you want to change into a frame.

2. Choose Element→Frame→Change To Frame.

NOTE   *To change any empty frame into a drawn object, select the frame with the Pointer tool and use Element→Frame→Change To Graphic.*

Gamut

The color gamut of a device is the range of colors that it can display. A typical computer monitor, which can produce millions of colors, has the greatest gamut, while most desktop printing equipment offers a significantly smaller range. Even so, inexpensive color printers can achieve some tones that monitors can't. Use a color management system (CMS) in PageMaker to display more consistent color between monitors and printers.

General Preferences; see Preferences

Graphics

Graphics are computer images, from photographs and illustrations to abstract shapes and logos. PageMaker allows you to place, or import, many different kinds of graphics files into your publication. You can also draw geometric shapes directly onto the Pasteboard with the Rectangle, Ellipse, Polygon, and Line tools in the PageMaker Toolbox.

You work with two broad categories of graphics in PageMaker: bitmap or raster graphics and vector graphics. In most publications, bitmaps are the more common of the two. Photographs are bitmaps, as are JPEG, TIFF, GIF, and BMP files. Vector graphics, such as EPS files, come from applications like Illustrator. Because of their makeup, vectors scale, or change size, much more reliably than bitmaps.

PageMaker gives you a modest set of commands for editing bitmap graphics. If you require more thorough processing, consider using an application such as Photoshop before placing the bitmaps in your publication.

Displaying Graphics

Speed versus quality: This is the classic trade-off in the world of computer design. If you want to display high-quality images on screen, your system may take a serious performance hit, especially if you use high-resolution bitmaps in your publication. To maximize system resources, you can change the way PageMaker displays your graphics on screen. To do so, choose File→Preferences→General from the PageMaker menu. Under Graphics Display, pick an option:

- Grayed Out causes your images to appear as featureless gray rectangles (see Figure G-1). This is the fastest setting.

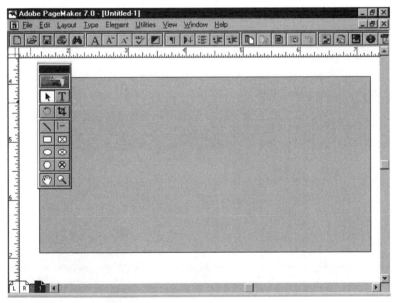

Figure G-1   PageMaker can gray out graphics.

- Standard, the default setting, gives you a fair representation of the actual image (see Figure G-2). If you look closely, your graphics may appear blotchy or distorted.

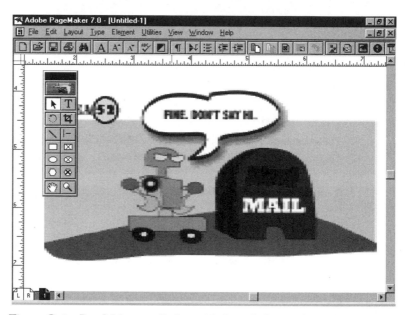

Figure G-2   PageMaker can display quick, low-resolution placeholder graphics.

- High Resolution presents your images with maximum sharpness and detail, but you may notice a drop in the performance of your system (see Figure G-3).

Figure G-3   PageMaker can display high-resolution graphics.

Please note that these options don't change the way that your images appear in print.

Modifying the Lightness and Contrast of a Monochrome or Grayscale Bitmap Graphic

To adjust the lightness and contrast of a bitmap graphic, select it with the Pointer tool and choose Element→Image→Image Control. The Image Control dialog box appears (see Figure G-4).

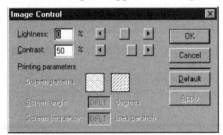

Figure G-4   The Image Control dialog box lets you tweak the appearance of a monochrome or grayscale image.

Drag the sliders to change the lightness and contrast: lightness affects the brightness or dimness of the image itself, while contrast controls its lightness or darkness in relation to the background.

Attaching a CMS Source Profile to a Color Bitmap Graphic

To associate a particular bitmap graphic in your publication with a CMS, select the bitmap with the Pointer tool and choose Element→Image→CMS Source. Define the source profile with the options in the CMS Source Profile dialog box (see Figure G-5). Please note that the image must be in color—it cannot be monochrome or grayscale.

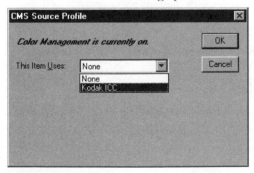

Figure G-5   Attach a source profile to a bitmap graphic with the CMS Source Profile dialog box.

Separating and Targeting Bitmap Graphics

Toward the end of a PageMaker project, if you plan to send your publication to a service provider, you should color-separate the non-CMYK bitmap graphics and target all bitmap graphics for the commercial printing equipment. To do so, make sure color management is on, and follow these steps:

1. Grab the Pointer tool from the Toolbox and select the bitmap that you want to separate and target.

2. Choose Element→Image→CMS Source and select the source profile of the output device on the CMS Source Profile dialog box. If the bitmap doesn't use a CMS, select one from the This Item Uses list and then choose the source profile. Click OK.

3. Choose File→Export→Graphic. The Export Graphic dialog box appears.

4. Choose a filename and location for the exported graphic, and save as type TIFF unless your service provider requests a different format. Don't save the same filename to the same location as the original graphic, or PageMaker gets upset.

5. Check the Save For Separation option. If the source profile matches the separation profile, PageMaker tells you about it and prevents you from saving the image for separation.

6. Click the Settings button, and choose Optimize For Separation from the Data Format list on the Export TIFF Options dialog box. You may adjust the other settings as required. Click OK.

7. Review the other options on the Export Graphic dialog box, and check those you need.

8. Click Save. Repeat this procedure for every bitmap in your publication.

TIP   *Specify a common filename prefix or suffix, like _sep, for all separated and targeted images. This way, when you use the Links Manager to review your graphics files, you can see at a glance the images that you still need to separate and target.*

Grouping Objects

In PageMaker, you can group objects together and manipulate them as a whole (see Figure G-6). Grouping is ideal when you finalize the layout of certain objects in relation to each other, such as the position of a text frame next to an image, but you still want to experiment with the layout of the page. Group the text frame and the image, and you can move them as a unit across the Pasteboard. In most regards, grouped objects behave as a single object.

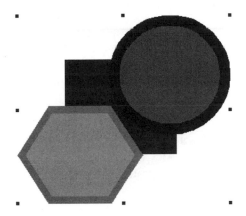

Figure G-6 When you group two or more objects, they act as a single object.

To group two or more objects, follow these steps:

1. Grab the Pointer tool from the Toolbox and select two or more objects.

2. Choose Element→Group.

To ungroup the objects, select the group with the Pointer tool and choose Element→Ungroup.

NOTE *You can group objects from multiple layers, but PageMaker automatically moves all the grouped objects to the layer of the uppermost object. If you ungroup the objects later, they don't return to their original layers.*

Guides

Use guides to build layout grids for precision alignment of your design elements. PageMaker provides three kinds of guides for your use:

- Column guides, which control the flow of text on the page
- Margin guides, which define the boundaries of the page
- Ruler guides, which allow you to align objects along horizontal and vertical straightedges

NOTE *A fourth type of guide, the baseline guide, is really just a horizontal ruler guide that the Grid Manager plug-in automatically positions for you.*

You can apply guides to any page. They appear on the Pasteboard, but they don't print out in your final publication.

Snapping Objects to a Guide

When you select and drag an object with the Pointer tool toward a guide, the object can snap, or align, to it. To enable this feature, follow these steps:

1. Select the View menu. If the Snap To Guides option doesn't have a check mark beside it, highlight this option and click.

2. To change the snap-to zone, or the range of the guide's snapping action, choose File→Preferences→Layout Adjustment. The Layout Adjustment Preferences dialog box appears. Supply a value for the snap-to zone and click OK.

Moving Guides

Use different commands to move different kinds of guides:

- To move column and ruler guides, first make sure that you haven't set the Lock Guides option under the View menu. Then, select the Pointer tool from the Toolbox. Click on the guide that you want to move and hold down the mouse button. Drag the guide across the page.

- To move margin guides, choose File→Document Setup. The Document Setup dialog box appears. Enter new values for the Inside, Outside, Top, and Bottom Margin fields. To reflow the text on the page, check the Adjust Layout option.

Locking Guides

You can lock guides to prevent them from moving after you place them. To turn on this feature, open the View menu. If the Lock Guides option doesn't have a check mark beside it, highlight this option and click (see Figure G-7).

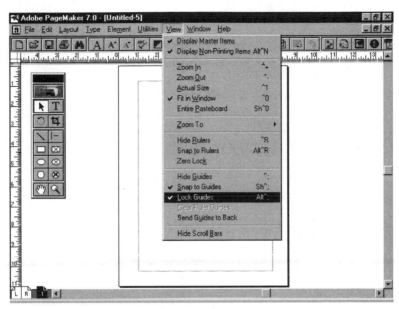

Figure G-7 Prevent guides from moving with the Lock Guides option.

Hiding Guides

To make the guides invisible, choose View→Hide Guides. To move the guides behind all objects on the page, choose View→Send Guides To Back.

Displaying Guides

To display the layout guides, choose View→Show Guides. To lay the guides on top of all objects on the page, choose View→Bring Guides To Front.

Removing Guides

Use different commands to remove different kinds of guides:

- To remove column guides, choose Layout→Column Guides. The Column Guides dialog box appears. Enter 1 in the Number Of Columns field.

- To remove margin guides, choose File→Document Setup. The Document Setup dialog box appears. Enter 0 for the Inside, Outside, Top, and Bottom Margin fields.

- To remove ruler guides, choose View→Clear Ruler Guides.

SEE ALSO *Columns, Layout Grids, Margins, Ruler Guides*

Hand Tool

Select the Hand tool from the Toolbox to move your view of the Pasteboard (see Figure H-1). When you click on the Hand tool, the mouse pointer changes into a hand icon. To use the tool, hold down the mouse button and drag. The Pasteboard moves in the direction that you move the mouse.

Figure H-1   Use the Hand tool to move the Pasteboard around the screen.

You can also use the Hand tool to find and follow hyperlinks. The hand icon changes into a finger when the mouse pointer passes over a hyperlink in your publication. To follow the hyperlink, click the mouse button.

Handles

Handles appear around an object when you select it (see Figure H-2). You can change the size and shape of the object by dragging the handles with the Pointer tool. To constrain the proportions of the object, hold down Shift while you drag the handles.

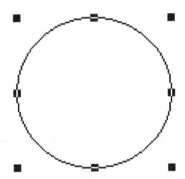

Figure H-2   This object has handles around it.

SEE **ALSO** *Windowshade Handles*

Hanging Indents

You have a hanging indent when a character or line sits outside the regular block of text, such as the bullet of a bulleted list (see Figure H-3).

Required listening

- *The Lamb Lies Down on Broadway* (Genesis)
- *Starless and Bible Black* (King Crimson)
- *Exotic Birds and Fruit* (Procol Harum)

Figure H-3   The bullets of this list hang outside the regular block of text.

To apply a hanging indent to a paragraph, follow these steps:

1. Grab the Text tool from the Toolbox. Click inside the paragraph to which you want to apply the hanging indent, or highlight a number of paragraphs.

2. Choose Type→Indents/Tabs. The Indents/Tabs ruler appears.

3. Click in the white space above the ruler to create a tab stop. Drag the tab stop to where you want to position the regular block of text.

4. Drag the position marker (the double-triangle icon) to where you want to place the hanging indent.

5. Hold down Shift, and drag the bottom triangle of the position marker to the same location as the tab you created in Step 3.

6. Click Apply. The Indent/Tabs ruler goes away.

7. The first line of the selected paragraph hangs. If you want to insert a character such as an item number, type the character at the beginning of the line and press Tab.

You can define hanging indents as part of a paragraph style, or you can use the default Hanging Indent style in the Styles palette.

SEE ALSO *Indents, Paragraph Styles*

Headers; see Running Headers and Footers

High-Fidelity Color

High-fidelity process color uses more than the four standard process-color inks (cyan, magenta, yellow, and black) to create a wider range of colors in printed publications. PageMaker provides two libraries of high-fidelity colors: Pantone Hexachrome Coated and Pantone Hexachrome Uncoated. Before you select from these libraries, be sure that your commercial printer can work with Pantone Hexachrome high-fidelity process color.

HLS

HLS stands for hue, lightness, and saturation. The HLS color model is an alternate method to RGB for defining on-screen colors. You can create colors in PageMaker using the HLS model.

Horizontal Scaling

PageMaker can change the horizontal scaling of text, making the characters wider or narrower (see Figure H-4).

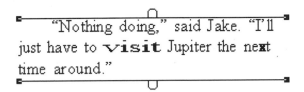

"Nothing doing," said Jake. "I'll just have to **visit** Jupiter the next time around."

Figure H-4   Which word has 200% horizontal scaling?

To change the horizontal scaling of text, follow these steps:

1. Use the Text tool from the Toolbox to select the character or range of characters that you want to scale.

2. Choose Type→Character. The Character Specifications dialog box appears.

3. Select a value from the Horiz Scale list, or type your own value in the field above the list, and click OK. The Character Specifications dialog box closes.

Horizontal scaling is a character-level attribute that you can set as part of a paragraph style.

SEE ALSO *Paragraph Styles*

HTML Files

HTML stands for Hypertext Markup Language, and HTML files contain the code for Web pages. When a browser like Internet Explorer or Navigator reads an HTML file, the application translates the HTML code into the Web page that appears in the main window. To see the HTML code itself, choose View→Source in Internet Explorer or View→Page Source in Navigator.

More specifically, the HTML code contains the text of a Web page, formatting information about the text, and instructions for the page layout. Web images don't reside in the HTML code the way copied graphics become part of your PageMaker publication. Instead, links in the HTML code point to another folder in the Web site, and that folder contains the image files.

PageMaker allows you to export your publication as a Web page. That means PageMaker creates an HTML file for the text, formatting, and layout of your page, and it saves your images as separate graphics files. When you open the HTML file in a Web browser, you see an approximation of your PageMaker publication. If your Internet service provider gives you personal Web space, you can post the PageMaker-generated HTML and graphics to the Web for all to see. Unfortunately, the more complex and design-intensive the publication, the less likely PageMaker can capture all the nuances of your work in HTML format. Also, PageMaker-drawn objects like ellipses and rectangles don't export to HTML at all. If you plan to create a PageMaker publication expressly for the Web, keep your design on the simple and elegant side, and use only placed graphics.

You can also import Web pages into PageMaker, although don't expect to see an exact reproduction of the page. You can reliably obtain text and graphics from the page, but you lose the majority of the layout.

TIP   *To ensure better translation of your publication to Web-page format, use PageMaker's default HTML paragraph styles. Open the Styles palette menu by clicking the triangle icon in the upper right corner of the palette, and choose Add Web Page Styles. If you don't see the Styles palette, go to Window@—>Show Styles.*

Exporting a Publication as a Web Page

Before you export your publication as a Web page, you may want to choose a Web browser in PageMaker's online preferences. This allows you to launch your browser automatically and view your Web page after the export finishes. If you don't select a Web browser in the online preferences, you can still export your publication as a Web page, but you must launch your browser manually to view the results.

To choose a Web browser in online preferences, follow these steps:

1. Choose File→Preferences→Online. The Online Preferences dialog box appears.

2. Locate the Web Browser field, and click the Browse button beside it.

3. Navigate to the browser program of choice. Windows users can find the Internet Explorer application under c:\Program Files\Internet Explorer\IEXPLORE.EXE. Locate Navigator 6 in c:\Program Files\Netscape\Netscape 6\NETSCP6.EXE. Double-click on the program icon.

4. Click OK in the Online Preferences dialog box.

To export your publication as a Web page, follow these steps:

1. Leave PageMaker for a moment, and create a folder to contain your Web page's images. Pick a convenient location on your hard drive, and plan to save your HTML file to the same place. Call the folder *img* or *images*.

2. Return to PageMaker, and choose File→Export→HTML. The Export HTML dialog box appears (see Figure H-5).

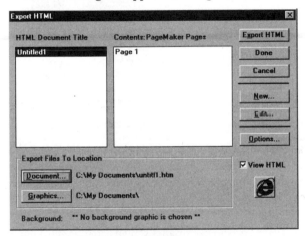

Figure H-5   Set up your publication for Web treatment in the Export HTML dialog box.

3. Click the title of the publication in the HTML Document Title window.

4. Under Export Files To Location, click the Document button. This calls the Document Save As dialog box. Navigate to the same location as the images folder from Step 1. Type a filename for the HTML and click OK. Leave the Save Images Into This Folder option unchecked.

5. Click the Graphics button. In the Browse For Folder dialog box, navigate to the images folder from Step 1. Select the images folder and click OK.

6. Click the Options button. The Export To HTML dialog box changes into the Options dialog box (see Figure H-6). Make sure you check the option for approximating the layout with tables. If you leave this option unchecked, the layout of your Web page won't resemble your publication.

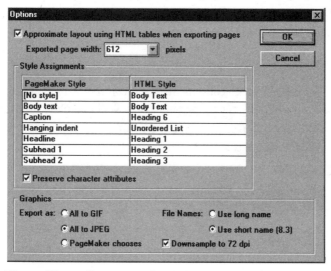

Figure H-6 Set options for the Web page in the Options dialog box.

7. Choose an exported page width. This is the width of the Web page in pixels. To estimate this number, take the width of the screen for which you're designing and subtract 30 pixels for vertical scrollbars, margins, and what not. For instance, if you design for a 640-width screen, set the exported page width to 610 pixels or so. You may design for a higher screen width, but visitors who use smaller screen settings get those annoying horizontal scrollbars in their browser window when they visit your page.

8. Under Style Assignments, review the conversion of your publication styles to HTML tags. If you know some HTML, you may modify these settings by clicking on a tag description in the HTML Style column. Otherwise, use the PageMaker default settings. Check the Preserve Character Attributes option to keep text formatting, such as bold and italic.

9. Under Graphics, select options for the Web page images. Remember, PageMaker saves the images as separate files, not as part of your HTML document. Stick with the default settings unless you have experience with preparing graphics for the Web.

10. Click OK in the Options dialog box. The Options dialog box changes back to Export To HTML.

11. Click the Edit button. The Export To HTML dialog box changes into the Edit Contents dialog box (see Figure H-7).

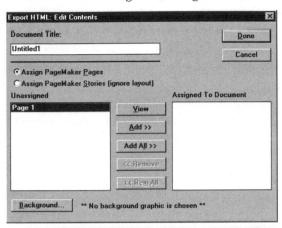

Figure H-7   Edit the content of the HTML file in the Edit Contents dialog box.

12. Give the Web page a title in the Document Title field. The title of a Web page appears at the top of the browser window.

13. Select between assigning PageMaker pages or PageMaker stories to the Web page. If you choose the option for stories, PageMaker ignores the layout of your publication and exports text only.

14. In the Assigned and Unassigned lists, click on the name of a page or story and move the item with the Add button or the Remove button. Assigned pages and stories appear in the exported HTML file. Unassigned pages and stories don't. Click View, and PageMaker turns to the specified page or story in the publication window. If you assign multiple pages or stories to export at the same time, PageMaker combines them all into a single Web page. If you want to create separate Web pages for each page or story in your publication, perform separate export operations.

15. Click the Background button to select a background graphic for the Web page. In the dialog box that appears, navigate to any GIF or JPEG image on your computer and double-click the icon. During the export, PageMaker drops a new copy of this graphic in the folder that contains the rest of your Web images. The background image tiles from left to right and top to bottom in a browser window. Pick a subtle image that won't distract from the text or make the Web page illegible.

16. Click Done. The Edit Contents dialog box changes back to Export To HTML.

17. If PageMaker's online preferences include your Web browser of choice, you may view your HTML file immediately after the export. To enable this, check the View HTML option. Change your Web browser preference by clicking on the browser icon and picking another program.

18. Click the Export HTML button. PageMaker informs you of any problems with the transfer. If you checked the View HTML option in Step 17, your browser program launches and loads the exported Web page.

NOTE   *If you export the Web page to a location that has spaces anywhere in its path name, such as c:\PageMaker\My Publications\Web, your browser may have problems automatically loading the exported file from PageMaker. To eliminate the risk, export the Web page to a folder on your desktop with no spaces in the name.*

Importing a Web Page

To import a previously saved Web page into PageMaker, follow these steps:

1. Create a blank PageMaker publication, or add a blank page to an existing publication.

2. Choose File→Place. Windows users can click the Place icon on the Toolbar. The Place dialog box appears.

3. Check the Show Filer Preferences option.

4. Navigate to the HTML file that you want to place, and double-click the icon.

5. The HTML Import dialog box appears. If you know HTML, you may want to fine-tune the conversion defaults between PageMaker styles and HTML tags. Otherwise, go with the PageMaker defaults.

6. Under Graphics, decide whether you want to import the images from the page or just the text. If you opt for images, select inline or independent graphics. Since PageMaker discards most of the Web page's layout during the import, you may question the usefulness of independent graphics.

7. Check the Keep Hyperlinks option if you want to preserve the coded HTML links in the imported Web page.

8. Click OK. When the import finishes, click Done to return to PageMaker.

TIP   *To import a Web page into PageMaker directly from the Web, click the Place URL button on the Place dialog box. For this to work properly, you may need to review your online preferences under File→Preferences→Online.*

Hyperlinks

In electronic publishing, a hyperlink is a pointer to information. Activate a hyperlink, and the target information appears, even if that information resides in some other document on the network. Few deny the power of this concept. How many computer books on your shelf come with cross-references to all the other computer books you own?

PageMaker allows you to embed hyperlinks in your publication. Your hyperlinks can point to anchors within your publication or URLs on the Web. PageMaker exports your hyperlinks with the rest of your publication when you save in PDF or HTML format, which means that you can distribute your publication electronically with all the links intact. You can also follow hyperlinks directly from PageMaker by using the Hand tool from the Toolbox.

Use the Hyperlinks palette to define the source of the link and its target (see Figure H-8). If you don't see the Hyperlinks palette, choose Window→Show Hyperlinks. Find additional commands and options in the Hyperlinks palette menu, which opens when you click the triangle icon in the upper right corner of the palette (see Figure H-9).

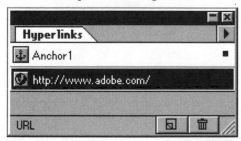

Figure H-8   The Hyperlinks palette gives you commands to add hyperlinks to your publication.

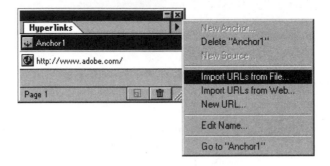

Figure H-9   Open the Hyperlinks palette menu by clicking the triangle icon.

Defining an Anchor

An anchor is a hyperlink target within your publication. To define an anchor, follow these steps:

1. Grab the Pointer tool from the Toolbox and select any object in your publication; or, using the Text tool, highlight any text.

2. Click the new-page icon at the bottom of the Hyperlinks palette. The new-page icon is next to the trashcan icon. The New Anchor dialog box appears (see Figure H-10).

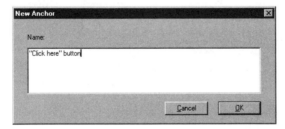

Figure H-10   The New Anchor dialog box lets you define an anchor.

3. Type a name or short description for the anchor and click OK. The Hyperlinks palette adds your anchor to the list. You may now link to this anchor from another place in your publication.

Defining a URL Destination

A URL destination is a hyperlink target on the Web. To define a URL destination, follow these steps:

1. Choose New URL from the Hyperlinks palette menu. The New URL dialog box appears (see Figure H-11).

Figure H-11 The New URL dialog box lets you define a URL destination.

2. Type the exact address of the destination in the URL field.

3. Click OK. The Hyperlinks palette adds your URL destination to the list. You may now link to this Web address from anywhere in your publication.

TIP   *Use mailto hyperlinks to send e-mail from your publication. When your readers click on the mailto hyperlink, their default e-mail client launches, and a blank message window opens with the e-mail address of your choice in the Send To field. To place a mailto hyperlink with PageMaker, define a URL destination as follows: "mailto:address@domain," where address@domain is the Send To e-mail address.*

Importing Hyperlinks from an HTML File on Your Computer

To import the hyperlinks from an HTML file on your computer, follow these steps:

1. From the Hyperlinks palette menu, choose Import URLs From File.

2. In the Import URLs dialog box (see Figure H-12), navigate to the HTML file that contains the hyperlinks that you want to import. Double-click the icon.

77

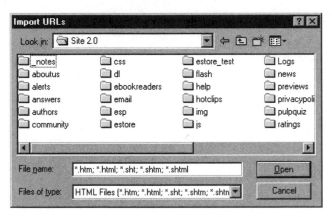

Figure H-12   Add URL destinations from a previously saved HTML file with the Import URLs dialog box.

3. The Hyperlinks palette adds all the URL destinations from the HTML file to the list.

Importing Hyperlinks from an HTML File on the Web

To import the hyperlinks from an HTML file on the Web, follow these steps:

1. Review your online preferences under File→Preferences→Online. Make changes as needed and click OK.

2. From the Hyperlinks palette menu, choose Import URLs From Web.

3. In the Place URL dialog box (see Figure H-13), type the entire address of the Web page that contains the hyperlinks that you want to import. Click OK.

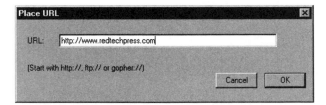

Figure H-13   Add URL destinations from a page on the Web with the Place URL dialog box.

4. PageMaker connects to the Web through your browser and transfers all the URL destinations from the Web page to the list on the Hyperlinks palette.

Setting the Source of a Hyperlink

The source of a hyperlink is the graphic or piece of text in your publication that the reader clicks to follow the link. To set a source, follow these steps:

1. Using the Pointer tool, click the graphic that you want to set as the source; or, using the Text tool, highlight the source text.

2. In the Hyperlink palette list, click the anchor icon or URL destination icon to which the source should link. The New Source dialog box appears.

3. Type a name or short description for the source and click OK.

Deleting a Hyperlink

To delete the source of a hyperlink, follow these steps:

1. In the Hyperlinks palette, click the source that you want to delete.

2. Click the trashcan icon in the bottom right corner of the Hyperlinks palette. PageMaker deletes the source, but the target anchor or URL destination remains in the list.

To delete the target of a hyperlink, follow these steps:

1. In the Hyperlinks palette, click the name of the anchor or URL destination that you want to delete.

2. Click the trashcan icon in the bottom right corner of the Hyperlinks palette. PageMaker deletes the target and all the sources linking to it.

In both cases, deleting a hyperlink doesn't remove the graphic or text that you set as the source or anchor. If you want to remove these items, select them with the Pointer tool and choose Edit@—>Clear.

NOTE   *If you delete the graphic or text of a hyperlink, the hyperlink breaks.*

Modifying a Hyperlink

To change the name of an anchor, double-click the anchor name in the Hyperlinks palette. To change the Web address of a URL destination, double-click the URL in the Hyperlinks palette. To change the source of an anchor or URL destination, first delete the current source in the Hyperlinks palette. Then, select a new source in your publication with the Pointer tool or the Text tool and click the new-page icon in the Hyperlinks palette.

Hyphenation

Hyphenation is the practice of breaking a word between syllables when it falls at the end of a line. PageMaker can automatically hyphenate your text, and you can control where, how, and how often. Use the Hyphenation command to set options for hyphenation (see Figure H-14).

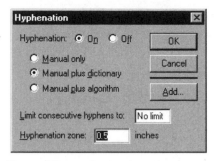

Figure H-14   Set hyphenation options with the Hyphenation dialog box.

The Hyphenation dialog box allows you to do the following:

- Turn hyphenation on or off by clicking the appropriate option button.

- Choose one of three hyphenation methods: Manual Only, Manual Plus Dictionary, and Manual Plus Algorithm. With Manual Only, PageMaker only hyphenates words that have user-defined discretionary hyphens. With Manual Plus Dictionary, PageMaker uses a built-in dictionary to determine where to break words. You may also manually set discretionary hyphens to break words that don't appear in the dictionary. With Manual Plus Algorithm, PageMaker refers to the built-in dictionary and observes your discretionary hyphens in addition to applying an algorithm, or set of rules, to figure out how to hyphenate the words that it doesn't recognize. If you select this method, keep in mind that the algorithm can make poor choices, so you may want to review the hyphenation yourself.

- If one line of text ends in a hyphen, and the very next line of text also ends in a hyphen, you have consecutive hyphens. Professional publishing tends to discourage these for aesthetic reasons, restricting the number of consecutive hyphens to two or three. Set your own limit by typing a value in the Limit Consecutive Hyphens To field. If you don't mind consecutive hyphens, type "No limit."

- As a line of type approaches the right margin of the text object, column, or page, any word that falls within the hyphenation zone is fair game for hyphenation. Increase or decrease the hyphenation zone by typing a value in the specified field. Please note that this option works only with unjustified text.

- Click the Add button to add a word to your user dictionary. Specify the new word in the Word field of the Add Word To User Dictionary dialog box. Insert a tilde (~) at a best-choice hyphenation break point. Insert two tildes at an average break point, and insert three tildes at an acceptable break point. If the word never breaks, insert no tildes. Choose a user dictionary from the Dictionary list, and click OK to add the word.

Hyphenating a Paragraph

To hyphenate a paragraph, follow these steps:

1. Grab the Text tool from the Toolbox and click anywhere inside the paragraph that you want to hyphenate, or highlight multiple paragraphs.

2. Choose Text→Hyphenation. The Hyphenation dialog box appears.

3. Set the options for hyphenation and click OK.

You can also set hyphenation as part of a paragraph style.

Inserting a Discretionary Hyphen

If you insert a discretionary hyphen in a word, PageMaker breaks the word at the hyphen when it needs to, and only when it needs to. If the word doesn't break, the discretionary hyphen doesn't appear. To insert a discretionary hyphen, Windows users should type a hyphen while holding down Ctrl+Shift. Mac users should type a hyphen while holding down Command+Shift.

TIP   *If you want the same word to break in the same place every time, add the word to your user dictionary.*

Inserting a Nonbreaking Hyphen

Normally, if a compound word like *high-five* falls at the end of a line, PageMaker breaks the line at the hyphen. If you don't want the compound word to split, insert a nonbreaking hyphen in place of the regular one. To insert a nonbreaking hyphen, Windows users should type a hyphen while holding down Ctrl+Alt. Mac OS users should type a hyphen while holding down Command+Alt.

Suppressing Hyphenation for One Instance of a Word

If you don't want a particular instance of a word to break, follow these steps:

1. Grab the Text tool from the Toolbar and click directly to the left of the word.

2. Windows users, hold down Ctrl+Shift while pressing the hyphen key. Mac users, hold down Command+Shift while pressing the hyphen key.

SEE ALSO *Paragraph Styles*

Importing; see Placing Objects

Imposition

To a commercial printer, an imposition is not just an unexpected houseguest. It is also an arrangement of several pages on a single sheet of paper. The imposition lays out the pages in such a way that, when the printer folds and binds the paper, the pages fall in correct running order. PageMaker's Build Booklet plug-in organizes your publication so that it prints as impositions.

Indents

Indents add space between the left or right margin of a text object and the beginning or ending of a line of type. PageMaker's Indents/Tabs ruler offers a quick and visual way to define indents (see Figure I-1).

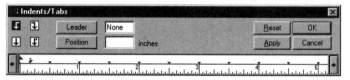

Figure I-1 Use the Indents/Tabs ruler to set indents.

On the Indents/Tabs ruler, in the white space above the numbers, notice the double-triangle icon pointing to the right and the single-triangle icon pointing to the left. The double-triangle icon marks the left indent, and the single triangle marks the right indent. Drag the icons along the ruler to position the indents.

The top triangle of the double-triangle icon marks the first-line indent, or the place where the first line of a paragraph begins. You can drag the top triangle independently of the bottom triangle; do this to set the first line further to the right than the rest of the paragraph.

Normally, when you drag the bottom triangle, the top triangle moves, too, even after you split them apart. If you want to drag the bottom triangle by itself, hold down Shift as you go. Using this method, you can create a hanging indent, where the first line of text begins further to the left than the rest of the paragraph.

To set an indent in a paragraph, follow these steps:

1. Grab the Text tool from the Toolbox. Click inside the paragraph to which you want to apply the indent, or highlight a number of paragraphs.

2. Choose Type→Indents/Tabs. The Indents/Tabs ruler appears.

3. Set the left, right, and first-line indents on the ruler.

4. Click Apply. The Indent/Tabs ruler goes away, and the selected paragraph indents.

You can also define indents as part of a paragraph style.

SEE ALSO *Hanging Indents, Paragraph Styles, Tabs*

Independent Graphics

An independent graphic is an image that you import directly into your publication with the Place command (see Figure I-2). You may move and manipulate an independent graphic without affecting any other design elements on the page. Compare this with the inline graphic, which sits inside a text object amidst running text.

Figure I-2   This image is an independent graphic.

Indexing

PageMaker can help you create an index for your publication. You build an index from a list of topics, or the words and phrases that your reader looks up. You can organize topics into levels, or subtopics. Each topic contains up to three levels. From these topics and subtopics, you create index entries, which direct your reader to a page or range of pages in your publication or a cross-reference to another topic.

Adding a Topic to the Index

To add a topic to the index, follow these steps:

1. Choose Utilities→Index Entry. The Add Index Entry dialog box appears.

2. Click the Topics button. The Select Topic dialog box appears (see Figure I-3).

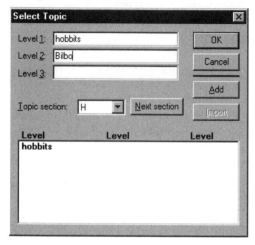

Figure I-3   The Select Topic dialog box allows you to define topics and subtopics for your index.

3. Type the level-one, level-two, and level-three topic categories in the Topic fields.

4. Click Add to add the topics to the index, or click OK to add the topics and close the Select Topic window.

5. Add an index entry, or click Cancel to close the Add Index Entry dialog box.

Adding an Entry to the Index

To add an entry to the index, follow these steps:

1. Using the Text tool, select the word or words that you want to add to the index.

2. Choose Utilities→Index Entry. The Add Index Entry dialog box appears (see Figure I-4).

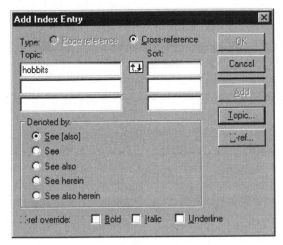

Figure I-4   The Add Index Entry dialog box lets you add an entry to the index.

3. Under Type, select Page Reference or Cross-Reference. A page-reference entry consists of the word from Step 1 followed by a list of page numbers on which the word appears. A cross-reference entry refers the reader elsewhere in the index.

4. Notice that there are three fields in the Topic area. These represent the three topic levels you can have in your index. The word you selected in Step 1 shows in the level-one field, meaning that the word generates a topic of its own in the index. If you want to add the word as a subheading in some other topic, click the promote/demote icon to place the word in the level-two or level-three field. Then, position the cursor in the level-one field and click the Topic button. The Select Topic dialog box appears. Choose a preexisting topic from the index by selecting the letter of the alphabet under which the level-one topic appears from the Topic Section list and clicking the topic name in the list. Create a new topic by typing topic names in the fields. Click OK in the Select Topic dialog box.

5. Notice that each Topic field has a corresponding Sort field. The Sort field for a topic tells PageMaker how to alphabetize the topic. For instance, if your topic is William Shatner, you probably want to sort it as "Shatner, William." To sort a topic differently than it appears in the Topic field, enter the sort spelling in the Sort field. Otherwise, keep the Sort field blank.

6. For a page-reference entry, the bottom half of the Add Index Entry dialog box lists the Page Range options. Select the option that best describes the coverage of the topic in the text. Choose the Current Page option if the current publication page discusses the topic and none of the other Page Range options apply. Choose the To Next Style Change option if the rest of the text in the current paragraph style discusses the topic. Choose the To Next Use Of Style option if all the text between the selected word and the use of a certain other paragraph style discusses the topic. Choose the For Next *x* Paragraphs option, and supply a number for *x*, to indicate the number of consecutive paragraphs that discuss the topic. Choose Suppress Page Range to supply no page numbers.

7. For a cross-reference entry, the bottom half of the Add Index Entry dialog box lists the Denoted By options. Select the type of cross-reference you want. Choose the See (Also) option if you want PageMaker to decide whether to use See or See Also. Choose the See option to supply a cross-reference with no page numbers of its own, such as "Captain Kirk. See Shatner, William." Choose the See Also option to supply a cross-reference in addition to a page reference. Choose the See Herein option to refer the reader to the level-two or level-three topics under another topic. Choose the See Herein Also option to refer the reader to the subtopics of another topic in addition to a page reference. After you choose the appropriate Denoted By option, click the X-Ref button to choose the topic to cross-reference. The Select Cross-Reference Topic dialog box appears (see Figure I-5). From the Topic Section list, choose the letter of the alphabet under which the level-one topic appears. PageMaker presents all the level-one topics that begin with this letter. Click the name of the topic that you want. You can also create a new topic by typing topic names in the fields. Click OK in the Select Cross-Reference Topic dialog box.

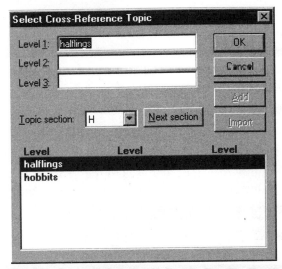

Figure I-5   Use the Select Cross-Reference Topic dialog box to define the cross-reference for your index entry.

8. Under Page # Override, choose formatting for the page range of the entry.

9. Click Add to add the current entry to the index, or click OK to add the current entry and close the dialog box. Use Add instead of OK when you want to add a similar entry to the index, such as a See Also cross-reference.

To add all occurrences of a keyword to the index at the same time, follow these steps:

1. Using the Text tool, click inside the story that you want to index.

2. Choose Edit→Edit Story. The Story Editor opens.

3. Choose Utilities→Change. The Change dialog box appears.

4. In the Find What field, type the keyword that you want to index as a level-one topic.

5. If you want to index all occurrences of this keyword, type a caret (^) and a semicolon (;) in the Change To field, like this: ^;. If you want to want to index all occurrences of this keyword as a proper name, such as "Lee, Stan" instead of "Stan Lee," type a caret (^) and a lowercase z in the Change To field, like this: ^z.

6. Click the Change All button. You may close the Change dialog box and the Story Editor.

You may also use keyboard shortcuts to index words as level-one topics. Highlight the word or phrase that you want to index and choose from the following list:

- To index the word, Windows users should press Ctrl+Shift+Y. Mac users should press Command+Shift+Y.

- To index the word as a proper name, Windows users should press Ctrl+Alt+Y. Mac users should press Command+Option+Y.

Reviewing the Index

To view and modify the index, choose Utilities→Show Index. The Show Index dialog box appears (see Figure I-6).

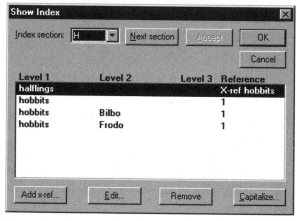

Figure I-6   The Show Index dialog box gives you commands for viewing and editing the index.

The Show Index dialog box gives you the following commands:

- In the Index Section list, choose the letter of the alphabet that you want to review.

- Click the Next Section button to jump to the next letter of the alphabet that contains index entries. This command skips letters that don't have any entries.

- Click the Add X-Ref button to add a cross-reference entry immediately after the currently highlighted entry. The Add Index Entry dialog box appears. Click X-Ref, fill in the cross-reference information in the Select Cross-Reference Topic dialog box, and click OK. The Select Cross-Reference Topic dialog box closes. Then click OK in the Add Index Entry dialog box and click Accept in the Show Index dialog box.

- Click the Edit button to modify the highlighted entry. The Edit Index Entry dialog box appears (see Figure I-7). Make changes to the entry and click OK. Then click Accept on the Show Index dialog box.

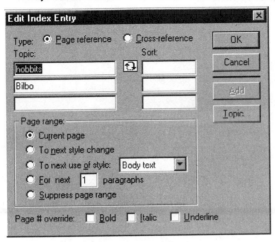

Figure I-7   Edit an index entry with the Edit Index Entry dialog box.

- Click the Remove button to delete the highlighted entry.
- Click the Capitalize button to control the first-letter capitalization of your index entries. In the Capitalize dialog box (see Figure I-8), choose to capitalize the first letter of the currently selected topic, all level-one topics, or all entries, and click OK.

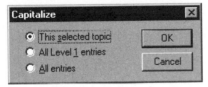

Figure I-8   Specify your capitalization preference for index entries in the Capitalize dialog box.

- Click the OK button to close the Show Index dialog box.

Placing the Index

To place the index text in your publication, follow these steps:

1. Choose Utilities→Create Index. The Create Index dialog box appears (see Figure I-9).

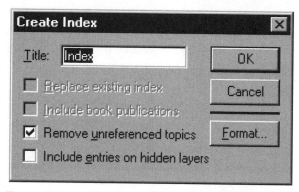

Figure I-9 The Create Index dialog box allows you to generate an index using the options you choose.

2. Supply a title for the index in the Title field.

3. To replace the current index with a new version, check the Replace Existing Index option.

4. If your publication has a book list, check the Include Book Publications option to create an index for the entire book. Please note that the book list must appear in all the book publications for this option to work properly.

5. To get rid of topics for which you have no page references or cross-references, check the Remove Unreferenced Topics option.

6. To include entries from text objects on hidden layers, check the Include Entries On Hidden Layers option.

7. To review the format of the index, click the Format button. The Index Format dialog box appears (see Figure I-10).

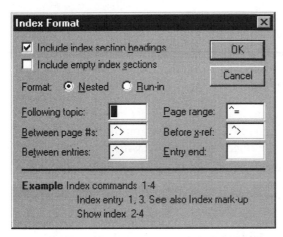

Figure I-10   Choose formatting preferences for your index in the Index Format dialog box.

8. The first two options concern section heads, or the letters of the alphabet that mark off the different sections of the index. If you want section heads, check the first option. If you want section heads for all letters of the alphabet, even if you have no entries for that particular letter, check the second option also. Under Format, choose between Nested and Run-In style: Nested style puts every entry on its own line, while run-in style separates entries with some kind of punctuation mark. Then, in the six format fields, type the characters and spaces you want to use to format the entries. You may enter multiple characters in the fields, and you may use PageMaker character codes for special typographical marks. Refer to the example area to see how your formatting choices look, and click OK to set your options.

9. Click OK in the Create Index dialog box. PageMaker compiles your index as a new story. The Create Index dialog box closes, and the mouse pointer becomes the loaded-text icon.

10. Turn on the Autoflow option in the Layout menu to place your index in a series of threaded text blocks. If you want to flow the index manually, or if you want to use text frames instead of text blocks, turn off this option.

11. Add a new page to your publication, or turn to the page where you want the index to begin. Select an insertion point on the page with the mouse pointer, and click the mouse button. The index appears in your publication.

Once you place the index, you may edit it by hand, just like any other text object, or you may repeat this procedure to make changes. Be sure to choose the Replace Existing Index option in Step 3.

Inline Graphics

An inline graphic is a graphic that sits inside a text object on a line of type (see Figure I-11). The inline graphic behaves much like a text character on the line. Compare this with the independent graphic, which is a separate object in the publication.

So, the robot   said, to no one in particular, "Hello!"

Figure I-11   This image is an inline graphic.

Jump Lines

In a publication like a newspaper, a jump line is a piece of text that directs the reader to the next page of the story, such as "Continued on page 5." If your story appears in text blocks, PageMaker can automatically add jump lines. To add jump lines to a story, follow these steps:

1. Grab the Pointer tool from the Toolbox and click the text block to which you want to add the jump line.

2. Choose Utilities→Plug-Ins→Add Cont'd Line. The Continuation Notice dialog box appears (see Figure J-1).

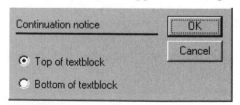

Figure J-1   Set jump lines with the Continuation Notice dialog box.

3. For a "Continued from" notice, select the Top Of Textblock option.

4. For a "Continued on" notice, select the Bottom Of Textblock option.

5. Click OK. PageMaker adds the jump line as a separate text block.

You may format and edit the jump line like any other text object.

TIP   *Only add jump lines once you finalize the layout of your publication. If you rearrange the text blocks of a story, the jump lines do not automatically update.*

Justification

If you add justification to a paragraph, all the lines of type in the paragraph become the same width. As a result, columns of text appear as blocks with clearly defined left and right margins. To achieve this effect, PageMaker adds space between the words of a line and sometimes between the individual letters in a word. Justification remains a hallmark of professional publishing, although unjustified, "ragged-right" style enjoys growing popularity.

There are two kinds of justification in PageMaker: justification (see Figure J-2) and force-justification (see Figure J-3). The Justify option justifies all full lines in the paragraph, but it leaves short lines alone. The Force Justify option justifies all lines, including short ones.

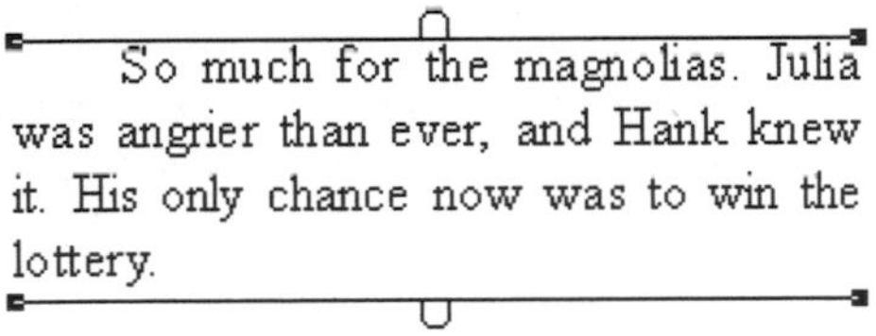

So much for the magnolias. Julia was angrier than ever, and Hank knew it. His only chance now was to win the lottery.

Figure J-2   This paragraph has justification.

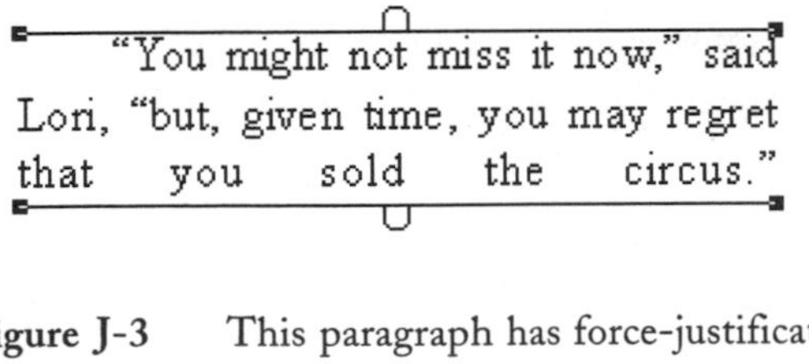

"You might not miss it now," said Lori, "but, given time, you may regret that   you   sold   the   circus."

Figure J-3   This paragraph has force-justification.

Justification happens according to the word- and character-spacing standards of the paragraph, which PageMaker defines as the minimum, desired, and maximum percentages of the normal spacing for the font. Change the minimum and maximum values of both character and word spacing to modify the way PageMaker justifies a paragraph. If you lower the minimum in relation to the desired value, you allow PageMaker to pack the line. If you raise the maximum value, justification creates looser-looking lines.

To justify a paragraph, follow these steps:

1. Grab the Text tool from the Toolbox. Click inside the paragraph that you want to justify, or highlight a number of paragraphs.

2. Choose Type→Paragraph. The Paragraph Specifications dialog box appears.

3. Under alignment, choose Justify or Force Justify.

4. To modify word- and character-spacing standards, click the Spacing button. The Spacing Attributes dialog box appears. Enter new values in the fields under Word Space and Letter Space, and click OK. The Spacing Attributes dialog box closes.

5. Click OK. The Paragraph Specifications dialog box closes, and the selected paragraph justifies.

Justification is a paragraph-level attribute that you can set as part of a paragraph style.

TIP   *When you use justification, also use hyphenation. This combination decreases the number of loose lines in your text.*

SEE ALSO *Paragraph Styles*

Kerning

Kerning is the space between two characters in a line of type. Compare this with tracking, which describes the looseness or tightness of the line of type as a whole. PageMaker expresses kerning as a positive or negative value. Positive kerning increases the space between characters, while negative kerning reduces the space.

Automatic Pair Kerning

Many fonts include information about pair kerning, or the proper spacing for certain pairs of characters, such as the uppercase *T* and lowercase *o* or the uppercase *W* and lowercase *e* (see Figure K-1).

Without this information, the word *We* appears to have too much space between the letters. PageMaker can apply automatic pair kerning to the text of an individual paragraph, or you can specify automatic pair kerning as part of a paragraph style. You can also specify a threshold point size, or the point size below which automatic pair kerning turns off. In most cases, you don't need pair kerning for very small text. The lowest threshold value is 4 points.

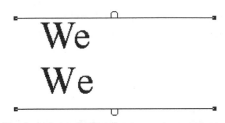

Figure K-1   This text block shows two pairs of letters, one with pair kerning, one without.

To set automatic pair kerning in a paragraph, follow these steps:

1. Grab the Text tool from the Toolbox. Click inside the paragraph, or highlight a number of paragraphs.

2. Choose Type→Paragraph. The Paragraph Specifications dialog box appears.

3. Click the Spacing button to open the Spacing Attributes dialog box.

4. Under Pair Kerning, check the option for Auto, and specify the threshold point size.

5. Click OK to close the Spacing Attributes dialog box, and click OK again to close the Paragraph Specifications dialog box.

NOTE   *To turn off automatic pair kerning, uncheck the Auto option in Step 4.*

Automatic pair kerning is a paragraph-level attribute that you can set as part of a paragraph style.

Manual Kerning

To apply kerning manually, follow these steps:

1. Grab the Text tool from the Toolbox and click between the characters you want to kern.

2. Locate the Control palette (see Figure K-2). If you don't see it, choose Window→Show Control Palette.

Figure K-2   The Control palette gives you manual kerning control.

3. Click the text icon on the Control palette. Find the kerning control on the far right of the palette, at the top.

4. Enter a value between −1.000 and 1.000 in the kerning field, or tap the arrow buttons to the left of the kerning icon to nudge the value in hundredth-point-increments.

Expert Kerning

PageMaker provides an Expert Kerning command for short blocks of display type such as headlines, slogans, and tag lines, when the spacing between characters must be perfect. You can only use expert kerning with PostScript fonts. If your Windows system has a preponderance of TrueType fonts, the PageMaker 7.0 Application CD comes with several high-quality PostScript fonts that you can install with the Adobe Type Manager 4.1 software, also on the CD.

To use expert kerning, follow these steps:

1. Grab the Text tool from the Toolbox and highlight the display type that you want to kern.

2. Choose Type→Expert Kerning. The Expert Kerning dialog box appears (see Figure K-3).

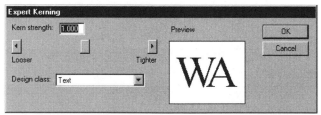

Figure K-3   Use the Expert Kerning dialog box for precise character spacing in display type.

3. Under Kern Strength, drag the slider toward a tighter or looser spacing preference. Watch the preview window.

4. Click OK to apply the kerning.

SEE ALSO *Paragraph Styles, Tracking*

Keylining Objects

A keyline is a visible border around an object, not unlike the stroke attribute that many objects possess (see Figure K-1). Unlike the stroke, though, PageMaker adds the keyline to your publication as a separate design element. Because of this, you can keyline any object in PageMaker, including text blocks and independent graphics, which don't have stroke attributes of their own.

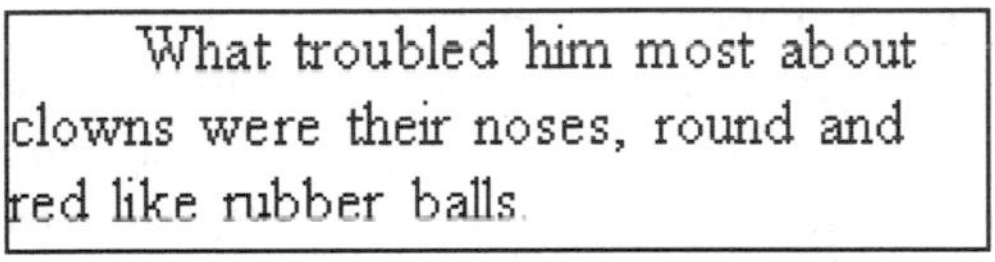

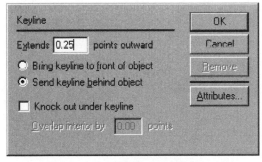

What troubled him most about clowns were their noses, round and red like rubber balls

Figure K-4   This text block has a keyline.

To keyline an object, select the object with the Pointer tool and choose Utilities→Plug-Ins→Keyline. The Keyline dialog box appears (see Figure K-5).

Figure K-5   The Keyline dialog box lets you add a keyline to an object.

Set the following options on the Keyline dialog box:

- Type a value in the Extends field to define how much space you want between the keyline and the object's contour.

- Choose to bring the keyline to the front of the object or send it behind the object by clicking the appropriate radio button. If you position the keyline in front of the object, the keyline may obscure it.

- Check the Knock Out Under Keyline option to knock out the colors underneath the keyline when you print your publication, and supply a value for how much to overlap the interior. If you don't check this option, the keyline overprints.

- Click the Attributes button to choose stroke and fill attributes for the keyline. Use this feature to make a dotted or dashed keyline or add a tint to a text block.

Click OK to set the keyline, or click the Remove button to delete the object's current keyline. To separate the keyline from its object, click the object with the Pointer tool and choose Element→Ungroup.

Knocking Out Color

If one colored design element sits on top of another color in the background and the background color doesn't print in the area where the two overlap, commercial printers say that the design element knocks out the background color. The opposite of knocking out is overprinting, where the entire background color prints, and the foreground color prints on top of it. Most elements in PageMaker knock out by default, with the exception of black text smaller than 24 points, which overprints. Check with your commercial printer to determine if you should overprint certain colors to avoid misregistration.

To cause an overprinting color to knock out, edit the color and remove the check mark next to the Overprint option. To cause black text to knock out, choose File→Preferences→Trapping and remove the check mark next to the Text Below x Pts. option under Auto-Overprint Black, or specify a new value for x.

Language Dictionaries

A language dictionary is the default PageMaker dictionary for a particular language. Every language dictionary has a user dictionary that contains a supplemental list of user-defined words.

For spell-checking and hyphenation purposes, each paragraph in your publication refers to a specific language dictionary. To change the language dictionary for a particular paragraph, select the paragraph with the Text tool. Then, choose Text→Paragraph to open the Paragraph Specifications dialog box. Pick a dictionary from the Dictionaries list, and click OK. If you have only one choice in the list, you can install additional language dictionaries from the PageMaker 7.0 Application CD. Having multiple dictionaries is helpful when you use more than one language in your publication.

SEE ALSO *User Dictionaries*

Layers

For convenience and control, organize your publication into layers. A layer is like a new, transparent Pasteboard that you pull over the current Pasteboard. You can position objects on the layer and manipulate them freely without disturbing the objects underneath. Transfer objects between layers with simple Copy and Paste commands. Show and hide layers with a single click, allowing you to test different foreground designs with a set background. You can create as many layers in your publication as you need.

When you work with layers in PageMaker, you use the Layers palette (see Figure L-1). If you don't see the Layers palette, choose Window→Show Layers. Access the most common layer commands with the icons at the bottom right of the palette. You can find additional layer commands in the Layers palette menu, which slides out when you click the triangle icon in the upper right corner (see Figure L-2).

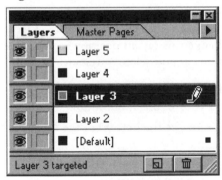

Figure L-1   The Layers palette lets you work with layers in PageMaker.

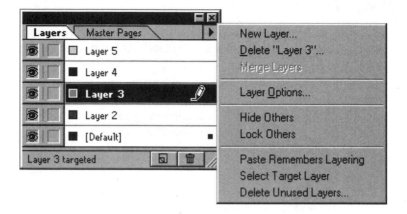

Figure L-2   Open the Layers palette menu by clicking the triangle icon.

Even if you didn't know about PageMaker layers before, you have been using them all along. Every publication has at least one layer, which PageMaker calls Default. You can add and remove objects from this layer, and you can change this layer's position relative to any others that you create, but you cannot delete or rename Default.

Creating a Layer

To add a new layer to your publication, follow these steps:

1. Click the new-page icon at the bottom of the Layers palette. The new-page icon is next to the trashcan icon. The New Layer dialog box appears (see Figure L-3).

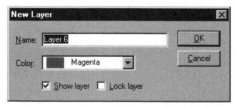

Figure L-3   Add a layer with the New Layer dialog box.

2. Type a name for the layer, and specify a color code from the Color list. When you place objects on the layer and select them with the Pointer tool, their handles appear in the color that you choose from the list.

3. To make your layer visible, check the Show Layer option. To make your layer invisible, leave this option unchecked. Please note that this choice isn't permanent. You can easily switch between layer visibility and invisibility on the Layers palette.

4. Don't check the Lock Layer option. Locking the layer prevents you from adding objects to it. Once you design the layer to your satisfaction, you can lock it.

5. Click OK. Your layer appears in the list on the Layers palette. To add objects to this layer, make sure that you select it from the list.

Hiding a Layer

To hide a layer, on the Layers palette, click the eye icon that corresponds to the layer you want to hide. The eye disappears, as do the contents of the layer (see Figure L-4). To make the layer reappear, click the empty eye-icon box.

Figure L-4   Hide a layer by clicking the eye icon.

To show or hide all the layers in a publication, open the Layers palette menu and choose Show All, Hide All, Show Others, or Hide Others.

Locking a Layer

To lock a layer, on the Layers palette, click the second box from the left next to the name of the layer you want to lock. The no-draw icon appears in the box, signifying that you cannot add objects, delete objects, or modify the current objects on the layer (see Figure L-5). Unlock the layer by clicking the no-draw icon.

Figure L-5   Lock a layer with the no-draw icon.

To unlock all the layers in a publication, open the Layers palette menu and choose Unlock All. To lock all but the currently selected layer, open the Layers palette menu and choose Lock Others. This command works only when all the layers are unlocked.

Deleting a Layer

To delete a layer, follow these steps:

1. On the Layers palette, select the layer that you want to delete.

2. Click the trashcan icon. The Delete Layer dialog box appears (see Figure L-6).

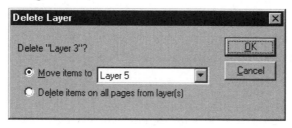

Figure L-6   Delete a layer with the Delete Layer dialog box.

3. You can choose to move the contents from the deleted layer to another layer in your publication, or you can delete all the layer's objects. Click the option button that corresponds to your choice.

4. Click OK.

To remove all empty layers from your publication, open the Layers palette menu and choose Delete Unused Layers.

Moving a Layer

On the Layers palette, you can drag a layer from one position in the list and drop it in another. A layer's position determines whether the objects in the layer appear above or below the objects in other layers, much like the stacking order determines what goes in front of what on individual layers.

Merging Layers

To merge two or more layers, from the Layers palette, select the layers that you want to merge. Windows users can select multiple layers by holding down Ctrl, while Mac OS users should hold down Command. Then, open the Layers palette menu and choose Merge Layers.

Selecting All the Objects on a Layer

To select all the objects on a layer, click the layer in the Layers palette. Then, open the Layers palette menu and choose Select Target Layer.

Moving an Object from One Layer to Another

To move an object from one layer to another, select the object with the Pointer tool and choose Edit→Cut. In the Layers palette, click the layer to which you want to move the object, and choose Edit→Paste.

If you don't want objects to switch layers during cut and paste, open the Layers palette menu and click the Paste Remembers Layering option.

Changing Layer Options

To change the name or color code of a layer, double-click the layer in the Layers palette. Reset the options in the Layer Options dialog box and click OK.

Layout Adjustment

PageMaker's layout adjustment feature helps you to reposition the objects in your publication after you modify the properties of the page. For instance, if you begin your design on a standard letter-size page with two columns but decide later that the page should be magazine size with three columns, layout adjustment nudges the elements in your design to match the new dimensions of the page, and, if you use text blocks, the text reflows to fit the new column scheme.

By default, PageMaker keeps layout adjustment off when you open a new publication. If you want to turn this feature on, choose File→Document Setup and check the Adjust Layout option.

To set the preferences for layout adjustment, follow these steps:

1. Choose File→Preferences→Layout Adjustment. The Layout Adjustment Preferences dialog box appears (see Figure L-7).

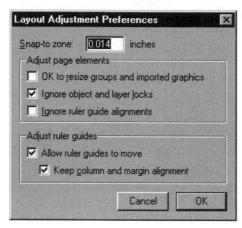

Figure L-7   The Layout Adjustment Preferences dialog box lets you modify the workings of layout adjustment in your publication.

2. Specify a snap-to zone. The snap-to zone is the area around a margin, ruler, or column guide by which the guide lays claim to an object. If an object falls within the snap-to zone of a guide, PageMaker assumes that the object belongs with the guide and moves them both when the page changes size. The larger the value in the Snap-To Zone field, the more likely PageMaker associates an object with a guide.

3. If you want PageMaker to resize group and image objects to fit the new layout, check the option for this. PageMaker maintains the aspect ratio of the resized objects, but bitmap graphics may appear distorted when you print them out, since bitmaps don't scale well.

4. If you want PageMaker to reposition locked objects, check the Ignore Object And Layer Locks option.

5. If you want PageMaker to reference margin and column guides only when deciding how to adjust your design, check the Ignore Ruler Guide Alignments option.

6. If you want ruler guides to move with the adjusted layout, check the option for this.

7. If you aligned ruler guides with your column and margin guides and you want these rulers to maintain their relationship with the columns and margins, check the Keep Column And Margin Alignment option.

8. Click OK to set the preferences.

Layout Grids

Layout grids improve the uniformity and precision of your publication's design. They consist of column, margin, and ruler guides, which appear on the screen but don't print in your final publication. PageMaker objects can snap, or attach themselves, to the guides, ensuring exact alignment of design elements.

In PageMaker, you can create layout grids manually by dragging column, margin, and ruler guides into your publication. You can also use the Grid Manager plug-in, which is less visual but generally faster (see Figure L-8). In addition, the Grid Manager allows you to set facing pages, or the left and right pages of a two-page spread, simultaneously.

TIP   *Apply layout grids to master pages instead of individual pages to promote design consistency.*

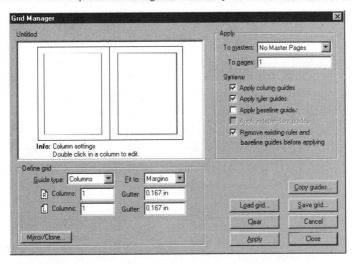

Figure L-8   Create a layout grid with the Grid Manager plug-in.

Creating a Layout Grid Manually

To create a layout grid manually, use column, margin, and ruler guides:

- To set column guides, choose Layout→Column Guides. In the Column Guides dialog box, supply the number of columns and the amount of gutter, or the space between the columns. Click OK.

- To set margin guides, choose File→Document Setup. Enter values for the inside, outside, top, and bottom margins in the Document Setup dialog box, and click OK.

- To create a ruler guide, locate the rulers along the top and down the left side of the screen. If you don't see them, choose View→Show Rulers. Position the mouse pointer in one of the rulers, hold down the mouse button, and drag a ruler guide into your publication.

Using the Pointer tool from the Toolbox, you can drag existing column and ruler guides anywhere you choose. Before you do this, check the View menu to make sure that you haven't locked the guides. If you see a check beside the Lock Guides option, highlight this option and click.

Creating a Layout Grid with the Grid Manager Plug-In

To create a layout grid with the Grid Manager plug-in, choose Utilities→Plug-Ins→Grid Manager. The Grid Manager dialog box appears. Note that the Grid Manager has four main divisions: the Apply area, the Define Grid area, the preview window, and the command buttons.

Under Apply, set the following options:

- Choose the master page spread or the individual pages to which you want to apply the layout grid. You can specify a range of pages in the To Pages field, separated by hyphens and commas, like this: 1-3, 5, 7-9, 11-.

- Under Options, check to apply column guides, ruler guides, and baseline guides. Baseline guides are horizontal ruler guides that PageMaker sets in relation to a leading value. To paste guides that you copied with the Copy Guides command, check the option for applying independent guides. To clear the current layout grid on the page when you apply the new grid, check the option for removing existing guides.

Under Define Grid, set the following options:

- From the Guide Type list, pick the kind of guide that you want to apply. The rest of the options in the Define Grid area change depending on the type of guide you choose.

- Select an option from the Fit To list. You can choose to align the guides with the page margins or the edges of the page.

- For column guides, set the number of columns and the amount of gutter, or the space between the columns.

- For ruler guides, set the number of vertical guides and the amount of gutter between columns, and the number of horizontal guides and the amount of gutter between rows. Note that horizontal ruler guides stretch across both pages, while you can apply vertical ruler guides to the left and right pages independently.

- For baseline guides, set the leading value in the Baseline Spacing field. PageMaker measures leading in points.

- Click the Mirror/Clone button to apply your grid to the spread in a variety of ways. Choose Right To Left With Mirroring or Left To Right With Mirroring to give the facing page the layout in reverse. Choose Right To Left or Left To Right to clone, or copy, the layout from one facing page to the other.

TIP   *What's the difference between column guides and vertical ruler guides? Column guides control the flow of text on the page, while ruler guides help you to align objects. If you want to flow text between multiple columns, use column guides. If you want to position design elements along a straight vertical line, use vertical ruler guides.*

Notice that the preview window changes as you define your layout grid. Double-click the preview window to make custom adjustments as you go:

- Select Columns from the Guide Type list and move the mouse pointer into the preview window. You may double-click a column to adjust its size relative to the other columns in the layout grid.

- Select Rulers from the Guide Type list and move the mouse pointer into the preview window. You may double-click a row to adjust its size relative to the other rows in the layout grid.

You may also use these commands:

- Click Copy Guides to copy the guides from the current left page, right page, or two-page spread. To paste these guides, enter the target page range in the To Pages field and check the Apply Independent Guides option.

- Click Save Grid to save the current layout grid as a Guides file. By default, PageMaker saves the Guides file to a subdirectory of the application folder, but you may choose any convenient location.

- Click Load Grid to load a layout grid that you previously saved.

- Click Apply to transfer the layout grid to your publication.

- Click Clear to remove all guides.

Layout View

Layout view is the default PageMaker user environment. It shows you the design of your page and allows you to manipulate design elements as objects. Compare this with the Story Editor environment, which looks and works more like a word processor. To return to layout view from the Story Editor, choose Edit→Edit Layout.

Modifying Layout View

If you work with multiple publications at the same time, you can modify the way that the layout view shows the windows. To display all publication windows on the same screen, choose Window→Tile (see Figure L-9). To position the publication windows one atop the other with visible title bars, choose Window→Cascade (see Figure L-10).

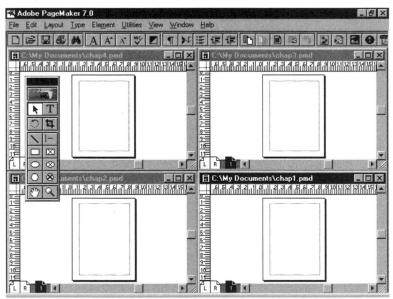

Figure L-9   PageMaker tiled these windows.

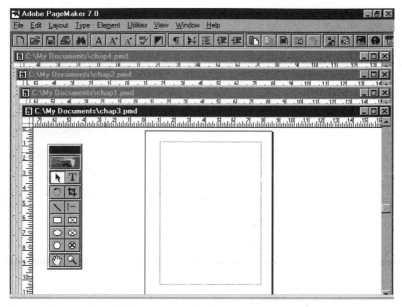

Figure L-10   PageMaker cascaded these windows.

Leading

Leading refers to the vertical space between lines of type (see Figure L-11). The term goes back to the days of manual typesetting, when printers inserted plugs of lead between rows to increase line spacing. You don't need a supply of lead plugs to use line-spacing controls in PageMaker.

Maybe he should have thought

twice about choosing the ostrich.

Amy certainly did. But once they got

him home, there was no turning back.

Figure L-11   This text block has 12-point type and 24-point leading.

Leading is a character-level attribute, which means that different characters in the same paragraph can have different leading values, even though the highest leading value in a line of type determines the size of the slug, or the vertical space that the leading creates.

To set the leading value, follow these steps:

1. Grab the Text tool from the Toolbox and select a character or range of characters.

2. Choose Type→Character. The Character Specifications dialog box opens. Type a leading value in the Leading field, or select a value from the drop-down list.

3. Click OK.

You can also set leading as part of a paragraph style.

Leading Methods

Unlike the leading value, which is a character-level attribute, the leading method, or the way in which PageMaker applies the leading, is a paragraph-level attribute. In other words, all lines in a paragraph use the same leading method, even if the leading values of individual characters differ.

Choose from three leading methods: proportional, top-of-caps, and baseline. Proportional leading, the default method, sets the baseline two-thirds of the way into the slug (see Figure L-12). Top-of-caps leading sets the top of the slug at the highest point of the largest character in the line of type (see Figure L-13). Baseline leading sets the baseline at the bottom of the slug (see Figure L-14). Giving adjacent paragraphs different leading methods increases or decreases the amount of space between the paragraphs.

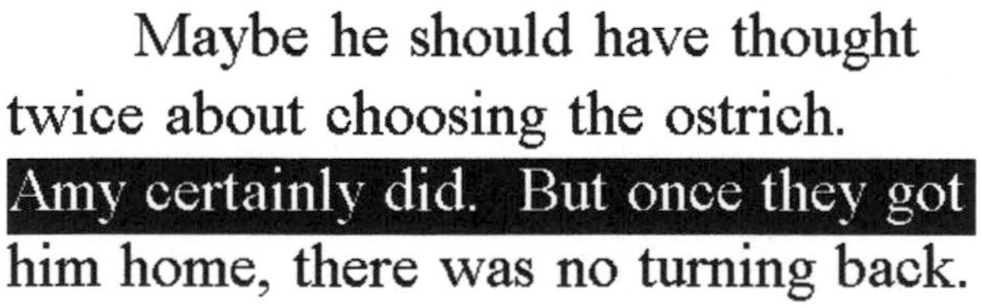

Maybe he should have thought twice about choosing the ostrich. Amy certainly did. But once they got him home, there was no turning back.

Figure L-12   This paragraph has proportional leading.

Maybe he should have thought
twice about choosing the ostrich.
Amy certainly did. But once they got
him home, there was no turning back.

Figure L-13 This paragraph has top-of-caps leading. Look carefully to
distinguish it from proportional leading.

Maybe he should have thought
twice about choosing the ostrich.
Amy certainly did. But once they got
him home, there was no turning back.

Figure L-14 This paragraph has baseline leading.

To set the leading method, follow these steps:

1. Grab the Text tool from the Toolbox and select a paragraph or a
   range of paragraphs.

2. Choose Type→Paragraph. The Paragraph Specifications dialog
   box appears.

3. Click the Spacing button. The Spacing Attributes dialog box
   appears.

4. Under Leading Method, choose the Proportional, Top Of Caps, or
   Baseline option and click OK. The Spacing Attributes dialog box
   closes.

5. Click OK in the Paragraph Specifications dialog box. The lines of
   the selected paragraph move in their slugs to reflect the new leading
   method.

You can also set the leading method as part of a paragraph style.

Autoleading

PageMaker expresses autoleading as a percentage of the character's
point size, and the default value is 120%. Therefore, if you use 12-point
type in the body text of your publication, the body-text leading becomes
14.4 points. Autoleading is a paragraph-level attribute, so different
paragraphs can have different autoleading settings.

111

To change the autoleading percentage, follow these steps:

1. Grab the Text tool from the Toolbox and select a paragraph or a range of paragraphs.

2. Choose Type→Paragraph. The Paragraph Specifications dialog box appears.

3. Click the Spacing button. The Spacing Attributes dialog box appears.

4. Under Autoleading, specify a new percentage, and click OK. The Spacing Attributes dialog box closes.

5. Click OK in the Paragraph Specifications dialog box.

You can also set Autoleading as part of a paragraph style.

SEE ALSO *Leading Grid, Paragraph Styles*

Leading Grid

A leading grid is a system of horizontal rules on the page, much like the lines on a piece of notebook paper, only invisible. The leading value of the body text determines how far apart these invisible rules are. For instance, if the leading value of the body text is 14.4 points, the rules of the leading grid are 14.4 points apart. Use a leading grid to make sure that the body text of your publication lines up properly in multicolumn text. To align text to a leading grid, follow these steps:

1. Using the Text tool from the Toolbox, click a paragraph whose text has a different leading value from the body text or a paragraph that has built-in space before or after it.

2. Choose Type→Paragraph. The Paragraph Specifications dialog box appears.

3. Click the Rules button. The Paragraph Rules dialog box appears.

4. Click the Options button. The Paragraph Rule Options dialog box appears.

5. Check the Align Next Paragraph To Grid option, and specify the precise leading of the body text in the Grid Size field. You can also pull down the Grid Size list to choose a leading value.

6. Click OK. The Paragraph Rule Options dialog box closes.

7. Click OK in the Paragraph Rules dialog box.

8. Click OK in the Paragraph Specifications dialog box. The paragraph immediately following the one that you selected in Step 1 aligns to the leading grid.

The Align Next Paragraph To Grid option is a paragraph-level attribute that you can define as part of a paragraph style. You can anticipate that headlines and styles that call for extra spacing before or after the paragraph are likely to diverge from the leading of the body text. Save yourself some time and set the Align Next Paragraph To Grid option as part of these styles.

Libraries

Libraries in PageMaker help you to organize frequently used objects and add them to your publication quickly. Open the Library palette to access your libraries (see Figure L-15). If you don't see the Library palette, choose Window→Plug-In-Palettes→Show Library. You can find commands and options for your libraries in the Library palette menu, which opens when you click the triangle icon in the upper right corner of the Library palette (see Figure L-16).

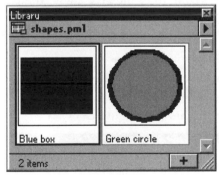

Figure L-15 The Library palette gives you access to frequently used PageMaker objects.

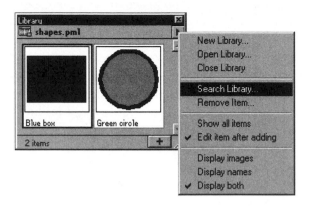

Figure L-16   Open the Library palette menu by clicking the triangle icon.

Once you create a library, you can drag items from the Library palette directly into your publication as new objects. You can then modify these objects without changing the properties of the library item. For instance, if your library contains a blue rectangle, you can drag an instance, or copy, of the blue rectangle into your publication and then change the color from blue to green. The library item remains blue.

Creating a Library

To create a new library file, follow these steps:

1. Choose New Library from the Library palette menu. The New Library dialog box appears (see Figure L-17).

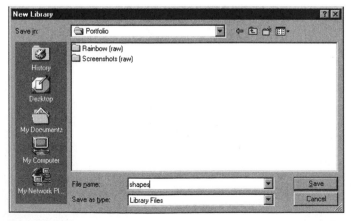

Figure L-17   Create a new library with the New Library dialog box.

2. Supply a name for your library in the File Name field, and choose a location on your computer to save the library file.

3. Click OK. PageMaker creates a new library file.

Adding an Object to the Library

To add an object to the library, follow these steps:

1. With the Pointer tool from the Toolbox, select the object that you want to add.

2. Click the plus button at the bottom of the Library palette. PageMaker adds the selected object as "Untitled."

3. Double-click the object thumbnail or name in the Library palette to open the Item Information dialog box (see Figure L-18).

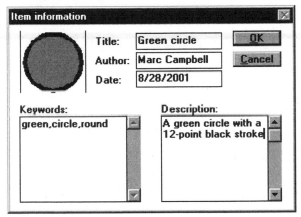

Figure L-18   The Item Information dialog box lets you add or edit information about a library object.

4. Fill in the Title, Author, Date, and Description fields, and provide search terms in the Keywords field. Separate keywords with commas and spaces.

5. Click OK.

Editing a Library Item

To edit the information of an item in the library, follow these steps:

1. Double-click the object thumbnail or name in the Library palette. The Item Information dialog box appears.

2. Update the information, and click OK.

Removing a Library Item

To remove an item from the library, follow these steps:

1. Click the object thumbnail or name in the Library palette.

2. Open the Library palette menu and choose Remove Item. PageMaker asks if you really want to remove the item from the library. Click OK to proceed.

NOTE   *The Are You Sure dialog box from Step 2 may appear as an error message. Don't worry about this—proceed normally.*

Searching the Library

To search the current library, follow these steps:

1. Choose Search Library from the Library palette menu. The Search Library dialog box appears (see Figure L-19).

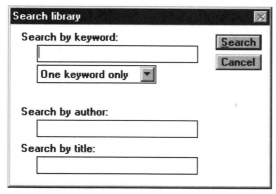

Figure L-19   The Search Library dialog box lets you scour your library by keyword, author, or title.

2. To search by keyword, type a search term in the Search By Keyword field. For a more advanced keyword search, select an operator from the drop-down list and supply the additional information in the second field that appears.

3. To search by author, type a search term in the Search By Title field.

4. To search by title, type a search term in the Search By Author field.

5. Click Search. Items that match all the search criteria appear in the Library palette. Drag the desired object into your publication.

6. To display all the items in the library, not just the search results, choose Show All Items from the Library palette menu.

TIP   *Narrow your search by supplying search terms in all the fields.*

Opening a Library

To open an existing library file, follow these steps:

1. Choose Open Library from the Library palette menu.

2. In the Open Library dialog box (see Figure L-20), navigate to the library file and click Open.

Figure L-20   Open a library with the Open Library dialog box.

Line Tool

Select the Line tool from the Toolbox to draw lines (see Figure L-21).

Figure L-21   The Line tool lets you draw lines.

SEE ALSO *Constrained-Line Tool*

Lines

To draw a line, follow these steps:

1. Select the Line tool from the Toolbox. The mouse pointer becomes a crosshairs.

2. Position the crosshairs where you'd like to start drawing, hold down the mouse button, and drag. You can adjust the size of the line as you go.

3. Release the mouse button (see Figure L-22).

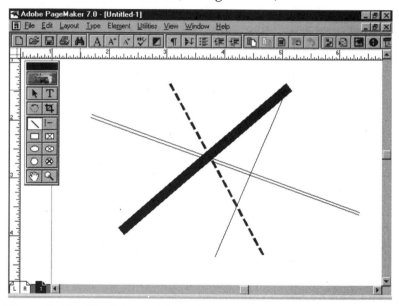

Figure L-22   The Line tool drew these lines.

To draw a horizontal, vertical, or diagonal lines at multiples of 45 degrees, select the Constrained-Line tool instead (see Figure L-23), or hold down Shift while drawing with the Line tool.

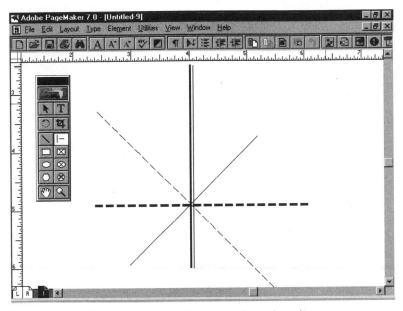

Figure L-23 The Constrained-Line tool drew these lines.

Linked Files

When you place a graphics file in your publication, PageMaker can link to the file's current location on your computer instead of making a copy of the file for the publication. Linked files show up in PageMaker as ordinary objects that you can move and manipulate just like the copied files. However, with linking, the file size of your publication can be drastically smaller, especially if you use high-resolution images. The drawback to using links is that the linked files must accompany your publication wherever it goes: to another computer, to a service provider, and so on. You must also take care not to move the files once you link to them, or PageMaker gets upset. For most designers, the benefits of linked files outweigh the risks. Once you get used to working with links, you may never go back.

By default, PageMaker always links to text files and never links to graphics files. You can change the way that PageMaker links to files by modifying the link options of your publication and its objects.

Changing Link Options

To change the link options of your publication, follow these steps:

1. Choose Utilities→Plug-Ins→Global Link Options. The Global Link Options dialog box appears (see Figure L-24).

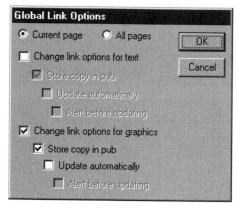

Figure L-24   Change settings for linked files in your publication with the Global Link Options dialog box.

2. Change the link options on the current page or throughout the publication by clicking the appropriate option button.

3. To modify text link options, check the Change Link Options For Text option. If you want PageMaker to update the file in the publication whenever you make changes to the original, check the Update Automatically option. If you want an alert message when this happens, check the Alert Before Updating option.

4. To modify graphics link options, check the Change Link Options For Graphics option. If you always want to link to graphics files, uncheck the Store Copy In Pub option. Check the options for updating the publication image if you want to activate these features.

5. Click OK.

To change the link options of an individual object, select the object with the Pointer tool and choose Element→Link Options.

NOTE   *You can't uncheck the Store Copy In Pub option for text files.*

Reviewing Linked Files

To review the files to which your publication links, follow these steps:

1. Choose File→Links Manager. The Links Manager dialog box appears, showing all the linked files in the current publication (see Figure L-25).

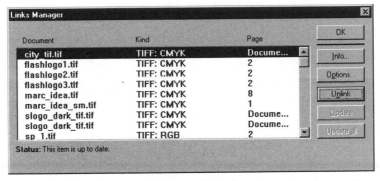

Figure L-25   The Links Manager dialog box lets you review and manage linked files.

2. Click on a file in the Links Manager dialog box.

3. If you see a question mark in front of the filename, it means that PageMaker can't find the linked file. Renaming or moving the file after you establish the link can cause this. To correct the problem, click the Info button and navigate to the linked file.

4. PageMaker tracks changes to your original files. Click Update or Update All to replace the linked files with updated versions. The Update button replaces the selected file only, while Update All replaces all out-of-date files in the publication. If you want PageMaker to update linked files whenever you make changes to the original, click the Options button and check Update Automatically.

5. If you want to remove the link entirely, click the Unlink button. PageMaker includes a copy of the file in your publication if necessary.

6. Click OK.

SEE ALSO *Copied Files*

Links; see Hyperlinks

Lists

To create a bulleted or numbered list, follow these steps:

1. Locate the Styles palette. If you don't see it, choose Window→Show Styles.

2. Select the Hanging Indent style, or choose your own style that has a hanging indent.

3. Create a new text object, or select an existing text object with the Text tool.

4. Type the list entries without bullets or line numbers. Press Enter after each entry. Make the list as complete as possible before you proceed, because bulleted and numbered lists in PageMaker can be difficult to edit.

5. Highlight all of the entries with the Text tool.

6. Choose Utilities→Plug-Ins→Bullets And Numbering. The Bullets And Numbering dialog box appears (see Figure L-26).

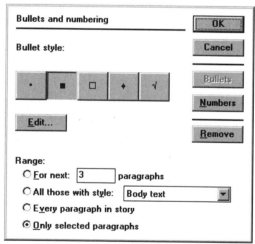

Figure L-26   Add bullets or numbers to a list with the Bullets And Numbering dialog box.

7. To make a bulleted list, click the Bullets button. To make a numbered list, click the Numbers button.

8. Choose a style for the list under Bullet Style or Numbering Style. For a numbered list, you may also select a separator character like a period or parenthesis and the starting number.

9. Under Range, choose Only Selected Paragraphs.

10. Click OK. Your list acquires bullets or numbers.

To edit the list, you may need to remove the bullet or number characters, make changes, and then reapply the plug-in.

SEE ALSO *Hanging Indents*

Locking Objects

After you finalize the position of an object, you can lock the object down to prevent it from moving. To lock an object, select it with the Pointer tool from the Toolbox. Then, choose Element→Lock Position. To unlock the object, select it again and choose Element→Unlock.

Loose Lines

Loose lines are lines of type with too much space between the words (see Figure L-27). PageMaker can highlight the loose lines in your publication if you choose File→Preferences→General and check the Show Loose/Tight Lines option.

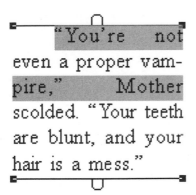

Figure L-27   These lines are loose.

SEE ALSO *Tight Lines*

Magic Stretch

PageMaker's magic stretch feature allows you to resize bitmap graphics in your publication while reducing loss of image quality. To use magic stretch, follow these steps:

1. Make sure that your publication's target output resolution is correct under File→Document Setup.

2. Using the Pointer tool from the Toolbox, select the bitmap that you want to scale.

3. While dragging one of the handles to scale the image, Windows users should hold down Ctrl, and Mac OS users should hold down Command. Hold down Shift as well to constrain the proportions of the graphic.

NOTE   *Don't be concerned if a magic-stretched graphic looks blurry on screen. The image still prints clearly.*

Magnify Tool

Select the Magnify tool from the Toolbox to zoom your view of the Pasteboard in or out (see Figure M-1).

Figure M-1   Zoom in and out with the Magnify tool.

Margins

The margins of your publication define the boundaries of the page. There are four margins in a two-page spread: inside, outside, top, and bottom. PageMaker represents these on the Pasteboard with margin guides, or pink lines (see Figure M-2). The margin guides don't print in your final publication, but you can make them invisible if they distract you by choosing View→Hide Guides.

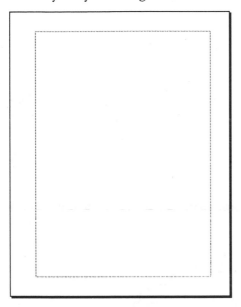

Figure M-2   These are margin guides.

To set or modify the margins of the page, follow these steps:

1. Choose File→Document Setup. The Document Setup dialog box appears.

2. Under Margins, type values in the Inside, Outside, Top, and Bottom fields. If you don't want margins on the page, type *0* in each of the fields. Please note that your desktop printer may have built-in margins that you can't override, and your external service provider undoubtedly charges extra for bleeds, or printing to the edge of the page.

3. Click OK.

NOTE   *If you work with single-sided pages, the inside and outside margins become left and right margins.*

TIP   *For better design consistency, define margins on master pages instead of individual publication pages.*

SEE ALSO *Guides, Layout Grids*

Masking Objects

When you mask an object, you create something like a window in front of it. You can see through the shape of the window to the object underneath, but you can't see the portion of the object that is outside the area of the window. To mask an object, follow these steps:

1. Locate the object that you want to mask in your publication.

2. Using the Ellipse, Rectangle, or Polygon tool, draw the shape of the window through which you want to see the object. The shape can have any kind of stroke attribute, but make sure the fill color is None.

3. Position the shape over the object that you want to mask.

4. Using the Pointer tool from the Toolbox, select both objects.

5. Choose Element→Mask.

6. Position the masked object exactly as you want it. Then, select both objects again, and choose Element→Group. You can now manipulate the masked object and the shape as a unit (see Figure M-3).

Figure M-3   The ellipse masks the image behind it.

To unmask an object, select it with the Pointer tool. Then, Windows users should press Shift, and Mac OS users should press Option. While holding down this key, choose Element→Unmask And Ungroup.

Master Pages

Master pages in PageMaker are like page templates. When you apply a master page to a publication page, the publication page acquires all the settings and design elements of the master. If you make a change to the master page, the publication pages that refer to it automatically update. Using master pages to control your design, you can generate highly consistent publications quickly.

When working with master pages, use the Master Pages palette (see Figure M-4). If you don't see the Master Pages palette, choose Window→Show Master Pages. You can find commands and options for master pages in the palette menu, which opens when you click the triangle icon in the upper right corner of the Master Pages palette (see Figure M-5).

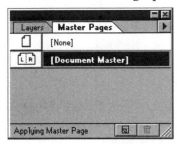

Figure M-4   The Master Pages palette allows you to define and apply master pages.

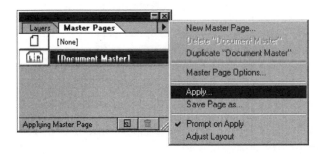

Figure M-5   Open the Master Pages palette menu by clicking the triangle icon.

All publications have at least one master page, which PageMaker calls Document Master. You can edit the settings of Document Master to suit your purposes, but you can't delete it. You can also create as many additional master pages as your publication requires.

To view a master page in PageMaker, click the L/R icon at the bottom left of the publication window. If you don't see the L/R icon, maximize the window. Then, in the Master Pages palette, click the name of the page that you want to view. To switch to another master page design, just click another name.

TIP   *On a publication page, to hide the design elements that come from the master page, uncheck the Display Master Items option under the View menu.*

Creating a Master Page

To create a new master page, follow these steps:

1. Click the new-page icon on the Master Pages palette. The new-page icon is at the bottom of the palette, next to the trashcan icon. The New Master Page dialog box appears (see Figure M-6).

Figure M-6   Create a master page with the New Master Page dialog box.

2. Type a name for the page, and choose whether to create a single page or a two-page spread.

3. Specify the margins by typing values in the Inside, Outside, Top, and Bottom fields. You can change these values later.

4. Under Column Guides, supply the number of columns and the width of the gutter, or the space between the columns. If you chose a two-page spread in Step 2, the fields on the left correspond to the left page, and the fields on the right correspond to the right page.

5. Click OK. The new master page appears in the list on the Master Pages palette.

To create a new master page from an existing publication page, follow these steps:

1. Turn to the publication page from which you want to create a new master.

2. Open the Master Pages palette and select Save Page As. The Save Page As Master dialog box appears (see Figure M-7).

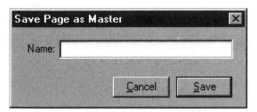

Figure M-7   Create a new master page from an existing publication page with the Save Page As Master dialog box.

3. Type a name for the new master page and click Save. The master page appears in the list on the Master Pages palette.

Designing or Editing a Master Page

To design or edit a master page, simply view the master page in PageMaker. Add objects or make changes to the master page exactly as you would for a regular publication page—all the commands and tools work normally. When you turn to a publication page that refers to your master, you won't be able to select or adjust the master-page elements.

To edit the name, margins, and columns of a master page, you can also choose Master Page Options from the Master Pages palette.

Applying a Master Page

To apply a master page to a publication page quickly, follow these steps:

1. If you want PageMaker to adjust the layout of the publication page after you apply the master, open the Master Pages palette menu. If Adjust Layout doesn't have a check mark in front of it, select this option.

2. Turn to the publication page to which you want to apply the master.

3. On the Master Pages palette, click the name of the master page that you want to apply.

TIP   *If you want the opportunity to cancel before PageMaker applies a master page, select Prompt On Apply from the Master Pages palette.*

For more options and better control, follow these steps:

1. Open the Master Pages palette and choose Apply. The Apply Master dialog box appears (see Figure M-8).

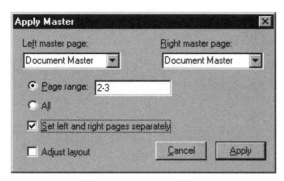

Figure M-8   Apply master pages to publication pages with the Apply Master dialog box.

2. Specify the page range over which you want to apply the master, or select the All option to apply the master to every publication page.

3. If you want to apply a separate master to the left and right pages in the page range, check the option for this.

4. Choose a master page from the Master list. If you checked the option to set left and right masters separately in Step 3, choose a left master and a right master.

5. Check the Adjust Layout option if you want PageMaker to reposition the elements in the publication pages to reflect the column and margin settings of the master.

6. Click OK.

NOTE   *If you apply a master page spread to a single publication page, the left page of the spread applies if the publication page is left facing, or even-numbered. The right page of the spread applies if the publication page is right facing, or odd-numbered.*

Deleting a Master Page

To delete a master page, follow these steps:

1. View the master page you want to delete.

2. Click the trashcan icon on the Master Pages palette.

Measurement Preferences

By default, PageMaker measures in inches. You can change this setting to millimeters, picas, ciceros, or points under File→ Preferences→General.

Mini-Save

A mini-save is a quick and rough save of your publication to your computer's hard drive. Certain commands cause PageMaker to do a mini-save automatically. You can initiate one yourself by clicking the active page icon at the bottom of the publication window. Use the mini-save feature to compensate for PageMaker's less-than-robust Undo command: Before making a significant alteration, mini-save your publication.

To revert to the most recent mini-saved version of your work, hold down Shift and choose File→Revert. Doing so discards any changes you made since the last mini-save.

TIP   *A mini-save may be good in a pinch, but it's no substitute for making permanent backup copies of your publications and storing them on separate media.*

Moving Objects

To move an object, click it with the Pointer tool from the Toolbox and hold down the mouse button until the mouse pointer changes into an arrowhead. Then, drag the object freely across the Pasteboard.

Negatives

A negative is a print with inverted colors. Be sure to find out if your service provider requires negative or positive images before you submit your publication as a PostScript file. To print your publication as a negative, choose File→Print and select your PostScript printer driver from the Printers list. Click the Color button, and check the Negative option.

Nonbreaking Characters

Characters such as spaces, hyphens, and forward slashes are fair game when PageMaker decides where a line of type should break. However, in some cases, you may not want a line to break at one of these characters. If so, you can insert a nonbreaking version of the character instead. PageMaker treats nonbreaking characters like letters—just as a line of type won't break between the letters of a word, the line won't break on either side of a nonbreaking character.

The following table shows PageMaker's nonbreaking characters and the key sequences you use to insert them:

CHARACTER	WINDOWS KEYS	MAC OS KEYS
Nonbreaking hyphen	Ctrl+Alt+-	Command+Option+-
Nonbreaking space	Ctrl+Alt+Spacebar	Command+Option+Spacebar
Nonbreaking forward slash	Ctrl+Alt+/	Command+Option+/
Em space	Ctrl+Shift+M	Command+Shift+M
En space	Ctrl+Shift+N	Command+Shift+N
Thin space	Ctrl+Shift+T	Command+Shift+T

NOTE *The backslash character (\) is always nonbreaking.*

Nonprinting Guides; see Guides

Nonprinting Objects

Normally, all objects within the margins of the page appear on paper when you print your publication. However, if you don't want a particular object on screen to print, select the object with the Pointer tool, pull down the Element menu, and check Non-Printing. Uncheck this option to cause the selected object to print.

NOTE *You can override the nonprinting setting, causing all objects to print as normal, under File→Print.*

Numbered Lists; see Lists

Numbering Pages

Use the page-number marker to add a page number to any page in your publication. Page-number markers automatically update themselves when you add or remove pages from your publication. To insert a page-number marker, follow these steps:

1. Create a new text object, or click an existing text object with the Text tool.

2. Position the cursor where you want to insert the page-number marker.

3. Windows users should press Ctrl+Alt+P. Mac users should press Command+Option+P.

Treat the page-number marker like any other character in the text object. Change the font and formatting, or apply a paragraph style. You can also add a prefix to the page number by typing the prefix before the page-number marker.

Change the style of the page numbers under File→Document Setup. Click the Numbers button in the Document Setup dialog box and choose a style. If you want to include your page-number prefix in the table of contents and index, enter the prefix in the TOC And Index Prefix field.

TIP   *Add the page-number marker to a master page for greater design consistency. All publication pages that refer to the master display and print with page numbers. When you add the page-number marker to a master page, the marker shows as LM on the left facing page or RM on the right facing page. Think of LM and RM as variables from algebra. When you view a publication page, PageMaker replaces LM and RM with the actual page-number values.*

Objects

Every image and text story in your publication is an object.

Selecting Objects

To select an object, click it with the Pointer tool. If you want to select the text of a text object, click the text object with the Text tool. To select multiple objects, hold down the Shift key as you click with the Pointer tool, or drag the Pointer tool to create a rectangular marquee. Releasing the mouse button selects every object inside the marquee.

Deleting Objects

To delete an object, select it with the Pointer tool and press the Delete key or choose Edit→Clear.

Cutting, Copying, and Pasting Objects

To cut an object, select it with the Pointer tool and choose Edit→Cut. To copy the object, choose Edit→Copy. To paste an object that you cut or copied, pick from the following commands:

• Choose Edit→Paste to paste one copy of the object.

• Choose Edit→Paste Multiple to paste more than one copy of the object. In the Paste Multiple dialog box, type the number of copies that you want. You can also give values for the horizontal and vertical offset of each successive copy, but these values aren't critical, since you can always move the pasted objects afterwards.

133

- Choose Edit→Paste Special to paste the object in a different file format. For instance, if you copy a text object, you can use Paste Special to paste the object in Rich Text Format instead of PageMaker format.

NOTE   *If you try to drag an item from a library after using the Paste Multiple command, PageMaker may become confused and add another pasted object to your publication instead of the library item. Set PageMaker straight by copying any object; then, drag from the library again.*

SEE ALSO   *Aligning and Distributing Objects, Arranging Objects, Coloring Objects, Graphics, Grouping Objects, Keylining Objects, Locking Objects, Masking Objects, Moving Objects, Placing Objects, Text Objects*

Online Preferences

To determine the style of electronic design elements like hyperlinks and establish the way that PageMaker communicates with the Internet, set or modify your online preferences. Review your current settings under File→Preferences→Online. This command opens the Online Preferences dialog box (see Figure O-1).

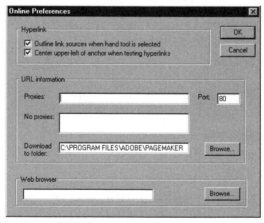

Figure O-1   Set online preferences with the Online Preferences dialog box.

From the Online Preferences dialog box, set the following options:

- Under Hyperlink, determine how hyperlinks should appear in your publication.
- The URL Information area requires technical details about your Internet connection. Obtain this data from your computer's settings, or check with your network administrator. If you leave these fields blank, PageMaker may have trouble connecting to the Internet.

- The Download To Folder field specifies where imported HTML files and graphics go before PageMaker gets to them. Pick a convenient location on your hard drive, or use the default setting.

- Select your Web browser preference. Click the Browse button next to the Web Browser field and navigate to your browser program. Windows users can find their browsers in the Program Files folder.

When you finish setting your online preferences, click OK.

Opening Publications; see Publications

Outline Fonts

Outline fonts are vector-based character sets, which means that they contain mathematical models of the shapes of the letters. Because of this, they scale, or change size, much more reliably than pixel-based bitmap fonts. Avoid bitmap fonts and use outline fonts like TrueType and PostScript Level 1 in your publication.

Overprinting

If a color prints on top of another color, you have overprinting. Compare this with knocking out, which happens when the foreground color replaces the background color where the two overlap. Your commercial printer may recommend overprinting to correct potential problems with color registration.

Colors knock out in PageMaker by default, with the exception of black text smaller than 24 points. To cause a knockout color to overprint, edit the color and check the Overprint option. To cause black strokes or fills to overprint, choose File→Preferences→Trapping and check the Strokes option or the Fills options under Overprint Black. To change the point size at which black text overprints, choose File→Preferences→Trapping, check the Text Below x Pts. option, and specify a new value for x.

Page Numbers; see Numbering Pages

Pages

To turn to a page, click the appropriate page icon along the bottom of the publication window. If you don't see the page icons, maximize the window. You can also choose Layout→Go To Page.

Adding Pages

To add pages to your publication, follow these steps:

1. Choose Layout→Insert Pages. The Insert Pages dialog box appears (see Figure P-1).

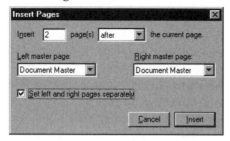

Figure P-1   Use the Insert Pages dialog box to add pages to your publication.

2. At the top of the dialog box, type the number of pages that you want to add and indicate where you want to add them.

3. From the Master list, pick the master page to which your new pages should refer. If you don't want a master page, select None from the list. If you plan to add more than one page, you can choose different masters for left facing and right facing pages. Check the Set Left And Right Pages Separately option, and then choose master pages from the lists.

4. Click the Insert button.

Removing Pages

To remove pages from your publication, follow these steps:

1. Choose Layout→Remove Pages. The Remove Pages dialog box appears (see Figure P-2).

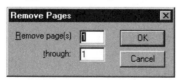

Figure P-2   Pare down your publication with the Remove Pages dialog box.

2. Type the range of pages that you want to remove.

3. Click OK. PageMaker asks if you really want to remove these pages and all of their content. Click OK to proceed.

Sorting Pages

To rearrange the pages in your publication, follow these steps:

1. Choose Layout→Sort Pages. The Sort Pages dialog box appears (see Figure P-3). Use the magnifying-glass icons to zoom the view in or out.

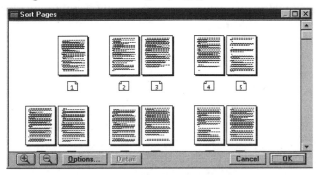

Figure P-3   You can rearrange your publication visually.

2. In the Sort Pages dialog box, select the thumbnail of the page or spread that you want to move. Note that when you click a spread, you select both pages by default. To select the left or right page only, Windows users should hold down Ctrl, and Mac OS users should hold down Command.

3. Hold down the mouse button and drag the selected page or spread to the desired place in the publication. If you want to insert the selected item between the left and right pages of spread, Windows users should hold down Ctrl, and Mac OS users should hold down Command.

4. Click OK.

Click the Options button to choose from the following:

- Check the Double-Sided option to reformat a single-sided publication as a double-sided publication. Uncheck this option to reformat a double-sided publication as a single-sided publication.

- If you check the Double-Sided option, you can also check the Facing Pages option to organize the publication into two-page spreads. Uncheck this option to organize the publication into individual pages.

- To see detailed thumbnail images of the pages, check the Show Detailed Thumbnails option. If you uncheck this option, the thumbnails become gray by default, but you can click the Detail button in the Sort Pages dialog box to see a detailed thumbnail of the currently selected page or spread.

- Check the Do Not Move Elements option if you don't want PageMaker to apply automatic layout adjustment to your publication when you change the first two options.

SEE ALSO *Master Pages*

Palettes

Palettes are the floating windows that contain commands and options for various PageMaker features. There are eleven palettes in all: Colors, Control, Data Merge, Hyperlinks, Layers, Library, Master Pages, Picture, Scripts, Styles, and Template. Having them all on screen at the same time could clutter the Pasteboard and interfere with your work. You can open or close any palette at will by pulling down the Window menu and selecting the palette to show or hide. Some of them appear under the Plug-In Palettes submenu. You might also find it helpful to group palettes together: Drag the tab of any palette into any other palette, and the palettes combine. To split grouped palettes apart, drag the tabs outside the palette window.

SEE ALSO *Control Palette, Picture Palette*

Pamphlets; see Books and Pamphlets

Paragraph-Level Attributes

Paragraph-level attributes are the characteristics of text that apply to paragraphs instead of individual characters. If you modify a paragraph-level attribute, all the text in the paragraph changes. Examples of paragraph-level attributes include alignment and tab stops. To review the attributes of a paragraph, select the paragraph with the Text tool and choose Type→Paragraph (see Figure P-4).

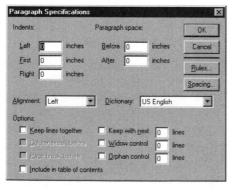

Figure P-4   Review paragraph-level attributes with the Paragraph Specifications dialog box.

SEE ALSO *Character-Level Attributes*

Paragraph Styles

A paragraph style is a collection of settings and attributes like font, leading, and alignment. When you apply a paragraph style to text, the text assumes the exact characteristics of the style, and, if you make changes to the style, the text automatically updates. However, the style/ text relationship doesn't work both ways: If you need to fine-tune the format of a certain piece of text, you can freely edit its properties without affecting the paragraph style. This kind of power makes it easy to control the format of the text in your publication.

Use the Styles palette to create, manage, and apply paragraph styles (see Figure P-5). You can find commands and options for paragraph styles in the Styles palette menu, which opens when you click the triangle icon in the upper right corner of the palette (see Figure P-6).

Figure P-5   Take charge of text formatting with the Styles palette.

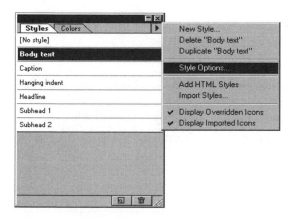

Figure P-6   Open the Styles palette menu by clicking the triangle icon.

139

PageMaker comes with several default paragraph styles, such as Body Text and Hanging Indent. These styles are ready to use when you launch PageMaker. When you first begin working with paragraph styles, rely on the PageMaker defaults. Once you get a feel for what styles can do and how they can help you, you can modify the defaults or define your own styles from scratch.

To apply a paragraph style, grab the Text tool from the Toolbox and click the paragraph that you want to style. Then, in the Styles palette, click the name of the style that you want to use. You can apply only one style to a paragraph at a time. For instance, if you use the Body Text style for a paragraph and you try to change a single sentence in the paragraph to Caption, the entire paragraph changes to the Caption style. However, you can always highlight the sentence and make changes to the formatting manually.

Defining a Paragraph Style

To define a paragraph style from scratch, follow these steps:

1. On the Styles palette, click the new-page icon. The new-page icon is next to the trashcan icon at the bottom of the palette. The Style Options dialog box appears (see Figure P-7).

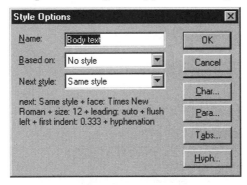

Figure P-7   The Style Options dialog box lets you define a paragraph style.

2. Type a name for the style in the Name field.

3. From the Based On list, select a style to use as the starting point for your new style.

4. From the Next Style list, choose the style that should automatically apply to the next paragraph when you press Enter at the end of the current paragraph.

5. Click the Char button to set character-level options like font and leading.

6. Click the Para button to set paragraph-level options like indents and alignment.

7. Click the Tabs button to set tab stops and hanging indents.

8. Click the Hyph button to control hyphenation.

9. Click OK in the Style Options dialog box. Your paragraph style appears in the list on the Styles palette.

To edit a paragraph style, double-click the name of the style in the Styles palette. This opens the Style Options dialog box and allows you to modify the settings. When you click OK, all the text that refers to the style updates automatically.

Deleting a Paragraph Style

To delete a paragraph style, go to the Styles palette and select the name of the style that you want to delete. Click the trashcan icon. Your publication does not change appearance, even if paragraphs refer to the deleted style. Affected text switches to the deleted style's Based On style, but it retains all the deleted style's formatting.

Duplicating a Paragraph Style

To duplicate a paragraph style, click the name of the style in the Style palette list and choose Duplicate Style from the Style palette menu. The Style Options dialog box appears. At your option, change the name and properties of the duplicate style.

Importing Paragraph Styles from a Publication

To import the paragraph styles from another PageMaker publication, select Import Styles from the Styles palette menu. In the Import Styles dialog box, navigate to the publication whose styles you want to import and double-click the icon. If an existing style in your publication has the same name as an imported style, PageMaker overwrites the existing style.

Importing Paragraph Styles from a Word-Processor Document

Word processors like Microsoft Word use styles very similar to PageMaker's. The styles are so similar, in fact, that when you place a word-processor document, PageMaker can import the style information with the text. To do so, make sure you check the Retain Formatting option in the Place dialog box.

Marking Up a Text File with Style-Name Tags

You can insert style-name tags in any text file using any text editor. When PageMaker imports text files that contain style-name tags, it can convert the tags into the specified styles for the paragraphs. To mark up a text file with style-name tags, follow these steps:

1. Launch your text-editing program, and open or create a new text file.

2. At the beginning of each paragraph, type the name of the PageMaker style that you want to apply to the paragraph. Put the style name between angle brackets (<, >). For instance, to mark a paragraph for the Headline style, type *<Headline>* at the start of the paragraph. The first word of the paragraph should come immediately after the closing angle bracket. Don't insert a space, and definitely don't press Enter.

3. Save your text file.

To import a marked-up text file into PageMaker, follow these steps:

1. Choose File→Place. Windows users can click the Place icon on the Toolbar. The Place dialog box appears.

2. Navigate to the marked-up text file, and click once on the icon to select it.

3. Check the Read Tags option.

4. Click Open.

Pasteboard

The Pasteboard is the work area in PageMaker's layout view.

PDF Files

PDF stands for Portable Document Format. This format preserves font, style, and layout information across different systems and platforms, which means that PDF files always look the same, no matter what kind of computer you use to view them.

PageMaker allows you to export your publication as a PDF file. Unlike exporting to HTML, exporting to PDF gives you a nearly identical reproduction of your work. However, before you can export to PDF, you need to install the following additional components from the PageMaker 7.0 Application CD:

- A PostScript printer driver and a PostScript Printer Description file (PPD), to print your publication to disk as a PostScript file
- Acrobat Distiller, to change the PostScript file to PDF format
- Acrobat Reader, to view the finished PDF file

You can also import pages from PDF files into your publication.

Exporting a Publication in PDF Format

To export a publication in PDF format, follow these steps:

1. Save your publication under File→Save, and then choose File→ Export→Adobe PDF. Windows users can click the PDF icon on the Toolbar. The PDF Options dialog box appears (see Figure P-8).

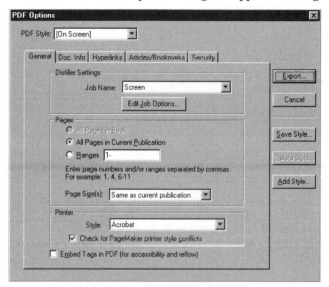

Figure P-8 Use the PDF Options dialog box to prepare your publication for PDF format.

2. Choose a PDF style from the PDF Style list. The On Screen style optimizes your PDF file for online distribution, but the file doesn't always print out clearly. The Print style creates a larger file, but it allows your audience to print out a better-looking hard copy. Many people prefer reading words on paper, so you might give the Print style some thought. You can import a previously saved custom style by clicking the Add Style button.

3. Review the general options. Under Distiller Settings, choose the Acrobat Distiller job option you want. In most cases, the Distiller setting should match the PDF style setting. That is, if you chose the On Screen style in Step 2, pick the Screen option from the Job Name list. If you chose the Print style, pick Print for desktop printers or Press for commercial printers. To review the Distiller settings, click the Edit Job Options button. If you make changes, you can save your settings as a custom job option. In the future, when you export to PDF, you can select your custom job option instead of the Distiller defaults.

4. Under Pages, determine the publication pages to export, and set the size of the exported pages.

5. Under Printer, choose the printer style you want to use for the export procedure.

6. Check the option for embedding tags to improve the readability of your PDF file in handheld devices and text-to-speech converters.

7. Click the Doc. Info tab and supply title, author, subject, and keyword information for the PDF file. The user accesses this information under File→Document Properties→Summary in Acrobat Reader 5.0.

8. A note is a kind of pop-up window that you can embed in PDF files. If you want to place a note on the first page of the file, type the text in the field under First Page Note and pick whether Acrobat Reader should open or close the note's pop-up window by default.

9. Click the Hyperlinks tab to determine how Acrobat Reader manages your publication's hyperlinks. By checking the Table Of Contents Links or Index Links options, you can automatically create hyperlinks to each item in your publication's table of contents or index. The External Links and Internal Links options preserve your publication's URL destinations and anchors, respectively. Change the appearance of the link under Default Appearance. The Magnification option allows you to set the way in which Acrobat Reader displays the target when a user follows a link.

10. Click the Articles/Bookmarks tab. Articles in PDF files are like stories in PageMaker publications: They don't have to flow from start to finish on consecutive pages. Defining articles helps the user to navigate the PDF file in Acrobat Reader. To set up articles, check the Export Articles option and click the Define button. The Define Articles dialog box appears (see Figure P-9). Click the List button to list all the PageMaker stories that meet the required number of text blocks. These are the stories that PageMaker converts to articles during the export. For more precise control, highlight an article in the list. Then, click the Edit button to add PageMaker stories to the article. Click the Remove button to prevent PageMaker from converting the story to an article. Click the Properties button to give the article its own title, subject, author, and keyword information. Click the New button to build an article from scratch using all available PageMaker stories in the publication.

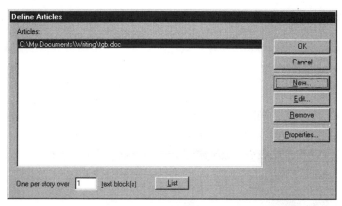

Figure P-9   Change your PageMaker stories to PDF articles with the Define Articles dialog box.

11. Bookmarks in Acrobat Reader appear on the left side of the document window. They work like hyperlinks, allowing the user to navigate the document easily. To make bookmarks from your table of contents or index, check the appropriate options.

12. Click the Security tab, and set password protection and editing privileges for the PDF file.

13. Click the Save Style button in the PDF Options dialog box to save the settings from all the tabs as a custom PDF style. In the future, when you export to PDF, your custom PDF style appears in the list with the PageMaker defaults.

14. Click the Export button.

15. Choose a name and location for the exported PDF file in the Export PDF As dialog box. If you want to launch Acrobat Reader and load the file immediately after the export, check the View PDF option. Click Save.

NOTE   *When you export your publication as a PDF file, you may notice inconsistencies between the page numbers that display in your publication and Acrobat Reader's built-in page-numbering system. To reconcile these differences, if you plan to distribute your publication as a PDF file, always begin the publication with page number one, even if the first page is a cover sheet.*

Importing a Page from a PDF File

You can import individual pages from a PDF file into PageMaker. Unfortunately, if you want to import the entire PDF file, you must do so one page at a time. To import a page from a PDF file, follow these steps:

1. Choose File→Place. Windows users can click the Place icon on the Toolbar. The Place dialog box appears.

2. Check the Show Filter Preferences option.

3. Navigate to the PDF file from which you want to import a page, and double-click the icon.

4. The PDF Filter dialog box appears (see Figure P-10). Pick the page you want to import, and set preview and print options.

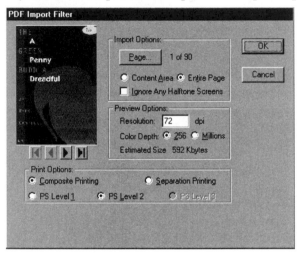

Figure P-10   The PDF Filter dialog box lets you import a page from a PDF file.

5. Click OK. PageMaker alerts you if a color in the PDF file conflicts with a color in your publication.

Photoshop Effects; see Adobe Gallery Effects

Pica

The pica is a unit of measurement in typography. One pica equals 1/6 inch and contains twelve points. The cicero is a slightly larger unit of measure that also contains twelve points.

SEE ALSO *Cicero, Point*

Picture Palette

The Picture palette gives you a ready stock of clip-art images to use in your publication (see Figure P 11). If you don't see the Picture palette, choose Window→Plug-In Palettes→Show Picture Palette. Browse the clip art by type and category to find the image you want. Then, drag the thumbnail into your publication. To place the image, you may need to insert the PageMaker 7.0 Content CD into your CD-ROM drive.

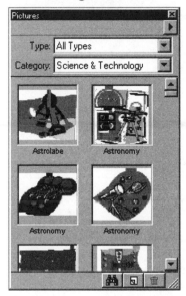

Figure P-11   Use the Picture palette to place PageMaker's clip-art images in your publication.

Find commands for reorganizing and adding your own images to the Picture palette under the Picture palette menu, which opens when you click the triangle icon at the upper right of the palette (see Figure P-12).

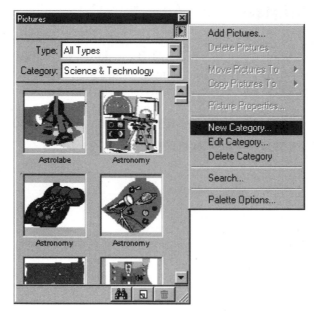

Figure P-12   Open the Picture palette menu by clicking the triangle icon.

NOTE   *When you use the Picture palette menu's Search command, your search results appear in the palette's category list under a user-defined criteria name. You can't perform a new search until you choose a different category.*

Placing Objects

Use the Place command to bring text and graphics files into your publication (see Figure P-13). You can place a file as a new, independent object, or you can import it into a frame. You can add the file to an existing object, or you can replace the object entirely.

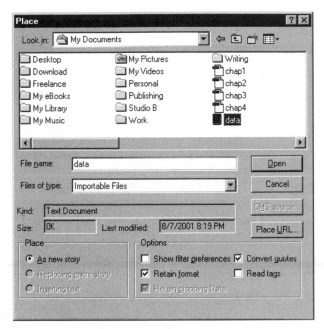

Figure P-13   Import text and graphics files with the Place dialog box.

Depending upon the kind of object you want to place, the options in the Place dialog box change. Set these under Place and Options. The Place area lets you determine how to place the file. The Options area gives you control over the import procedure. Choose from the following options:

- Check Show Filter Preferences for a dialog box that allows you to choose additional settings for the type of file you want to place.

- For text files, check Retain Format to import paragraph styles and other formatting in a word-processor document. Check Convert Quotes to change typewriter-style quotes into typographer-style smart, or curly, quotes. Check Read Tags to import style tags. Style tags are like HTML tags in many respects. They appear between angle brackets (<, >) at the beginning of a paragraph, and they denote the style that PageMaker should apply to the paragraph. For instance, to mark a paragraph for Body Text style, <Body Text> should appear at the beginning of the paragraph. If you check this option, PageMaker converts style tags to the appropriate formatting. If you don't check this option, the tags have no effect on paragraph styles, and they appear with the words in the imported text file.

149

- For graphics files, check Retain Cropping Data if you want to replace a cropped image in your publication with a new graphics file but you want to keep the crop information.

You may opt to place a link to the file instead of a copy of the file itself. Linking to files can significantly decrease the file size of your publication, especially if you use high-resolution images. Set options for linking under Utilities→Plug-Ins→Global Link Options.

To place an object, follow these steps:

1. Choose File→Place. Windows users can click the Place icon on the Toolbar. The Place dialog box appears.

2. Navigate to the file that you want to place, and click the icon once to select it.

3. Set the options in the dialog box according to your preferences.

4. Click the Place button.

Placing an Object in a Frame

To place an object in a frame, draw the frame, or select an existing frame with the Pointer tool. Then, choose File→Place.

Placing a Text File in an Existing Text Object

To place a text file in an existing text object, grab the Text tool from the Toolbox and select an insertion point or highlight the text that you want to replace. Then, choose File→Place.

Placing an Inline Graphic in a Text Object

To place an image as an inline graphic, create a new text object, or pick an insertion point in an existing text object with the Text tool. Choose File→Place, and select As Inline Graphic.

Replacing an Existing Object with a Placed File

To replace an existing object with a placed file, select the object with the Pointer tool. Then, choose File→Place.

Point

The point is the smallest typographical unit of measure. There are twelve points in both picas and ciceros. A pica-point equals 1/72 inch, and the slightly larger cicero-point equals 0.376 mm. When many sources, including this book, discuss points, they mean specifically pica-points.

SEE ALSO *Cicero, Pica*

Pointer Tool

Use the Pointer tool from the Toolbox to select objects in your publication (see Figure P-14).

Figure P-14   The Pointer tool lets you select objects.

Polygon Tool

Use the Polygon tool from the Toolbox to draw polygons and stars (see Figure P-15).

Figure P-15   Draw polygons and stars with the Polygon tool.

Polygons and Stars

To draw a simple polygon or a star, follow these steps:

1. Select the Polygon tool from the Toolbox. The mouse pointer becomes a crosshairs.

2. Position the mouse pointer where you want to start drawing, hold down the mouse button, and drag. Adjust the size and the shape of the polygon as you go (see Figure P-16). Pressing Shift while you draw constrains the proportions of the shape.

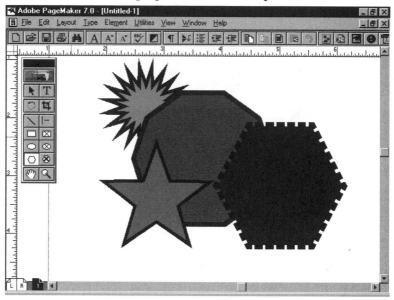

Figure P-16   The Polygon tool drew these simple polygons and stars.

3. Release the mouse button.

4. To change the number of sides of the polygon or transform the polygon into a star, choose Element→Polygon Settings.

To draw a complex polygon, follow these steps:

1. Select the Polygon tool from the Toolbox. The mouse pointer becomes a crosshairs.

2. Position the mouse pointer where you want to start drawing, and click and release the mouse button.

3. Move the mouse to draw the first side of the shape. Hold down Shift to constrain the angle to multiples of 45 degrees.

4. Click the mouse button to start a new side, and continue drawing. You can add as many sides to the shape as you like.

5. To finish, join the end point of the last side to the start point of the first. A small square appears at the intersection. Click the mouse button, and the shape closes (see Figure P-17).

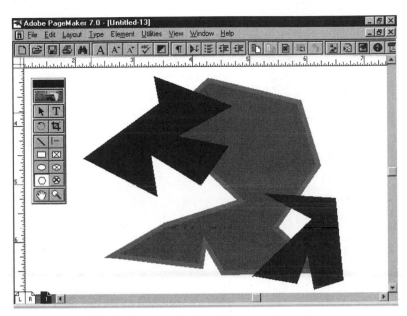

Figure P-17   The Polygon tool drew these complex polygons.

PostScript Files

If your commercial printer doesn't have access to PageMaker 7.0 for your specific platform, you can hand off your finished work as a PostScript file instead. PostScript files contain all the information that your service provider needs to print your job. In some respects, PostScript files are more complete than native PageMaker publications. However, you must ensure that the PostScript file contains correct information, because the printer isn't able to modify the file settings as easily as those of a PageMaker publication. Check with your service provider before generating a final PostScript file, and, no matter how you decide to submit your publication, always, always, always save a copy for yourself in PageMaker format.

To create a PostScript file of your publication, choose File→Print. The Print Document dialog box appears. Select a PostScript printer from the Printer list, and click Options. Check the Write PostScript To File option, and choose the type of PostScript file you want to create: Normal (.ps), EPS (.eps), or Separation (.sep). Specify a name and location for the PostScript file, and click Save.

TIP   *Use the Save For Service Provider plug-in to check your PostScript file before sending it off to the printer. Choose Utilities→Plug-Ins→Save For Service Provider, and click the Preflight .ps button to open your PostScript file. Then, click the tabs in the Save For Service Provider dialog box to review the file settings.*

NOTE   *Acrobat Distiller changes PostScript files to PDF files. If you save a PostScript file of your publication, you can feed it to Acrobat Distiller manually as an alternative to the Export→Adobe PDF command.*

PostScript Printer Description Files; see PPD Files

PPD Files

PPD stands for PostScript Printer Description, and a PPD file contains technical specifications about your PostScript printer. PageMaker needs the correct PPD for your hardware in order to print to it.

Even if you don't own a PostScript printer, PageMaker requires that you install PPDs on your computer to save PostScript files for your service provider or create PDF files for electronic distribution. If you plan to submit your publication to a commercial printer as a PostScript file, make sure you obtain the correct PPD for the printer's equipment. The PageMaker CD contains generic PPDs that allow you to export your publication in PDF format.

Preferences

Choose File→Preferences→General to set the general preferences of your publication. This opens the Preferences dialog box (see Figure P-18).

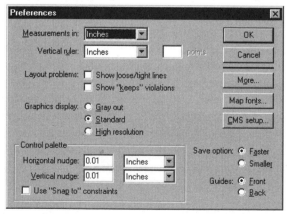

Figure P-18   Use the Preferences dialog box to set preferences for your publication.

Then choose from the following options:

• Set the unit of measure with the Measurements In list.

- You can set the unit of measure for the vertical ruler independently of the rest of the publication by selecting an option from the Vertical Ruler list. If you choose Custom, enter a point value in the field next to the list to create a leading grid.

- Check the Layout Problems options to highlight loose and tight lines or show instances where PageMaker can't keep desired lines of text together.

- Determine how PageMaker presents images under Graphics Display.

- Set options for the Control palette.

- Under Save Option, choose Faster for better speed but larger file size. Choose Smaller for slower speed but more compact file size.

- Under Guides, choose where column, margin, and ruler guides should display: in front of all objects or behind all objects.

Click the Map Fonts button in the Preferences dialog box to modify the way PageMaker replaces missing fonts on your computer, and click the CMS Setup button to turn on color matching and set CMS preferences. Click the More button to open the More Preferences dialog box (see Figure P-19).

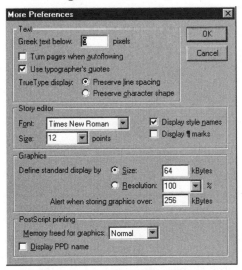

Figure P-19 Set additional preferences for text and graphics with the More Preferences dialog box.

Then set the following options:

- Determine the point size at which PageMaker greeks, or grays out, text on screen. No matter how the text displays, it prints normally.

- Check the Turn Pages When Autoflowing option to view each new page that PageMaker adds to your publication during an Autoflow procedure. The pages may flash by briefly, but you will see them all. If you don't check this option, PageMaker jumps you to the last page automatically.

- Check the Use Typographer's Quotes option to turn on smart quotes.

- Under TrueType Display, PageMaker can preserve your publication's leading by reducing the shape of an oversized character in a TrueType font, or it can preserve the shape of the oversized character at the risk of it crashing into other lines of type.

- Set options for the Story Editor.

- Under Graphics, the Standard Display option determines the quality of on-screen images when you select the Standard option for graphics display in the Preferences dialog box. The higher the file size or resolution percentage, the better the images appear on screen. This option has no effect on the quality of the images as they print out.

- The Alert When Storing Graphics Over x KBytes field shows the threshold for PageMaker's copy-versus-link trigger: If a graphics file exceeds this size, PageMaker asks if you want to place a link instead of a copy of the file.

SEE ALSO *Measurement Preferences, Online Preferences, Trapping*

Preview Mode

PageMaker's preview mode allows you to follow hyperlinks in your PageMaker publication (see Figure P-20). To enter preview mode, simply select the Hand tool from the Toolbox. The mouse pointer changes into the hand icon, and PageMaker temporarily outlines the hyperlinks in your publication with a blue box. Move the hand over a hyperlink, and the icon changes into a finger. Click the mouse button, and PageMaker follows the link. To return to the page with the hyperlink, choose Layout→Go Back. If the hyperlink goes to the Web, PageMaker launches the browser program that your online preferences specify.

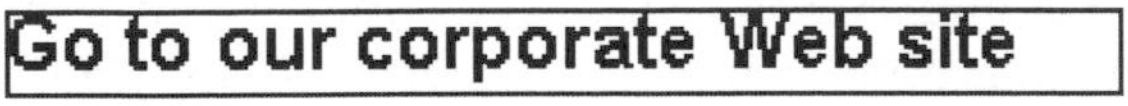

Go to our corporate Web site

Figure P-20   In preview mode, you can see borders around hyperlinks.

Under File→Preferences→Online, you can change the way that preview mode works. In the Online Preferences dialog box, uncheck the option for outlining links to suppress the blue outline. The hand icon still changes to a finger, even if you disable the outline option. Also, PageMaker automatically puts the upper left corner of the anchor in the center of the publication window when you follow the hyperlink. If you would rather have the target page display normally, uncheck this option.

Printer Styles

A printer style is a collection of print settings that you can use to switch among different kinds of print jobs quickly. To define a printer style, follow these steps:

1. Choose File→Printer Styles→Define. The Define Printer Styles dialog box appears (see Figure P-21).

Figure P-21   The Define Printer Styles dialog box lets you manage printer styles.

2. Select a printer style on which to base your new style, and click the New button. Type a name for the style in the Name Printer Style dialog box, and click OK.

3. Click Edit in the Define Printer Styles dialog box. The Print Document dialog box appears.

4. Set your printer options, and click OK.

5. Click OK in the Define Printer Styles dialog box.

Printing a Publication Using a Printer Style

To print a publication using a printer style, choose File→Printer Styles, and select the style that you want to use. The Print Document dialog box appears with the settings of the style. Click Print.

Removing a Printer Style

To remove a printer style, choose File→Printer Styles→Define. Highlight the style on the Define Printer Styles dialog box, and click Remove.

Printing Publications; see Publications

Process Color

Standard process color uses four separate plates for four separate inks—cyan, magenta, yellow, and black—to reproduce color in print. Use process color for most purposes in a full-color publication.

Proofs

Proofs are rough printouts of your publication. Proofing your work on a desktop printer gives you an idea about what your publication will look like when it comes back from the service provider. PageMaker gives you several proofing choices in the Print Options dialog box, which opens when you select File→Print. Review the following options:

- To print empty-frame placeholders instead of graphics, click the Document button and check the Proofs option.

- To print reader's spreads, which have two publication pages per sheet of paper, click the Document button and check the Reader's Spreads option.

- To print thumbnail versions of the publication pages, click the Options button and select Thumbnails. Then, specify the number of thumbnails that you want per page.

- To print printer's marks, crop marks, or publication information, click the Options button and check the appropriate boxes.

- To print grayscale in place of color, click the Color button and, under Composite, choose Grayscale. To print solid black in place of color, choose Print Colors In Black.

Proxy

The Proxy is the icon on the Control palette that allows you set a reference point (see Figure P-22). The Control palette takes all its measurements from this point, which corresponds to the same point on the selected object. For instance, if you select an image with the Pointer tool and choose the upper left corner of the Proxy as the reference point, the Control palette measures the size and position of the image from the upper left corner. If you go on to choose the middle right point of the Proxy, the Control palette measures the image from the middle right and changes its values accordingly.

Figure P-22 The Proxy determines the Control palette's reference point.

There are two kinds of reference points in PageMaker: absolute reference points, which don't change position as you modify an object; and relative reference points, which do change position. Absolute reference points appear as large squares on the Proxy. Relative reference points appear as arrows. To set a reference point, click one of the small squares on the Proxy. To change the reference-point type, click again on the same Proxy square.

SEE ALSO *Control Palette*

Publication Pages; see Pages

Publications

A publication is a PageMaker document. Find commands for creating, printing, and saving publications under the File menu.

Creating a New Publication

To create a new publication, follow these steps:

1. Choose File→New. Windows users can click the new-page icon on the Toolbar. The Document Setup dialog box appears (see Figure P-23).

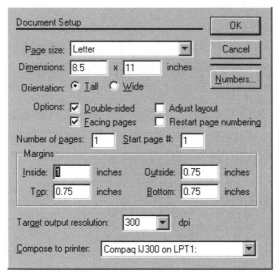

Figure P-23   Set up your publication with the Document Setup dialog box.

2. Set the page and margin options for your publication, and select the printer you plan to use and the resolution at which you intend to print. You may update these choices at any time by selecting File→Document Setup.

3. Click OK.

Opening a Publication

To open a publication, follow these steps:

1. Choose File→Open. Windows users can click the open-folder icon on the Toolbar. The Open Publication dialog box appears (see Figure P-24).

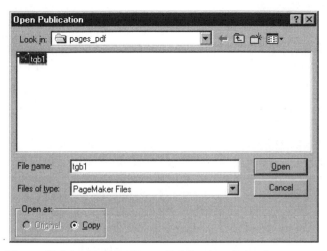

Figure P-24   Use the Open Publication dialog box to open a
PageMaker file.

2. Navigate to the publication that you want to open, and click the icon
to select the file.

3. Under Open As, select Original to open the publication under the
original filename. Select Copy to open the publication in a new,
untitled window.

4. Click Open.

Printing a Publication

To print a publication, follow these steps:

1. Choose File→Print. Windows users can click the printer icon on the
Toolbar. The Print Document dialog box appears (see Figure P-25).

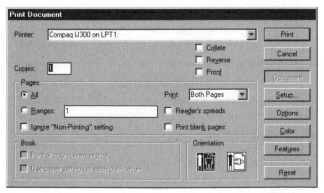

Figure P-25   Print a publication from the Print Document dialog box.

2. In the Print Document dialog box, select the printer that you want to use. For best results, this printer should match the one that you specified in the Document Setup dialog box when you created the publication. If you select a PostScript printer, choose a PPD file from the PPD list.

3. Type the number of copies that you want to print, and check the Collate option to collate them.

4. Check the Reverse option to print a negative. Check the Proofs option to print placeholders instead of graphics. Check the Ignore "Non-Printing" Setting option to print all objects in your publication, including nonprinting ones. Check the Reader's Spreads option to print two publication pages per sheet of paper. Check the Print Blank Pages option to include publication pages that have no objects.

5. Under Pages, choose the page range that you want to print, and, from the Print list, specify the kinds of pages to print. The Both Pages option prints all pages. The Even Pages option prints only even-numbered pages, and the Odd Pages option prints only odd-numbered pages.

6. Under Book, if you want to print all the publications in the current book list, check the Print All Publications In Book option. If you print to a PostScript printer, check the Use Paper Settings Of Each Publication to allow the other publications to override the current paper settings.

7. Under Orientation, click the icon on the left to print portrait-style, or click the icon on the right to print landscape-style.

8. Click the buttons on the right to review more print options. These options depend on the capabilities of your printer. The Setup button opens your printer's dialog box. The Options button lets you change the page scale, print crop marks, and do similar tasks. The Color button allows you to set options for color printing: Choose Composite to print a full-color or grayscale version of your publication, or choose Separations to print separate pages for each color plate. Click Reset to go back to the default print settings. If you use a PostScript printer, the Paper button replaces the Setup button. Click Paper to select the paper size. The Features button gives you access to whatever additional PostScript printing controls that your printer and PPD support.

9. Click Print.

NOTE   *Composite printing doesn't show trapping, knockouts, and overprints. Print separations to check these.*

TIP   *If you turn on color management in your publication, you can print separations of RGB images. Without color management, RGB images appear as grayscale on the Black plate of the separation.*

Saving a Publication

To save a publication, follow these steps:

1. Choose File→Save. Windows users can click the floppy-disk icon on the Toolbar. The Save Publication dialog box appears (see Figure P-26).

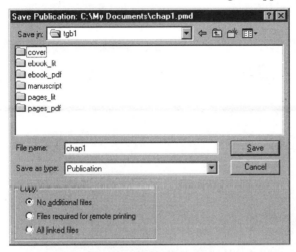

Figure P-26 The Save Publication dialog box lets you save your work.

2. Type a filename, and choose a convenient location to save the file.

3. Select the Publication option from the Save As Type list.

4. Under Copy, choose the No Additional Files option to save only the PageMaker publication. Choose the Files Required For Remote Printing option if you want to save your publication for use on another computer. This option makes copies of all the necessary files for printing and saves them in the same place as your publication. Choose the All Linked Files option to save copies of all linked files in the same place as your publication.

5. Click Save.

To save a publication under a different filename or in a different location, choose File→Save As.

TIP   *Use the Save As command whenever you want to save your publication with the smallest possible file size. The Save command is faster, but it creates a larger file.*

163

Saving a Publication for a Service Provider

If you plan to deliver your work to a commercial printer, use the Save For Services Provider plug-in. This plug-in helps to ensure that you include all the required information, and you can use it to troubleshoot and correct printing problems. To use the Save For Services Provider plug-in, follow these steps:

1. Save your publication with the File→Save or File→Save As command.

2. Choose Utilities→Plug-Ins→Save For Service Provider. The Save For Service Provider dialog box opens (see Figure P-27).

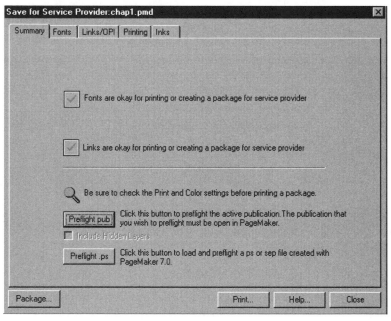

Figure P-27   The Save For Service Provider plug-in helps you package your publication for a commercial printer.

3. Click the Preflight Pub button.

4. Read the information under the Summary tab. Then, click the other tabs to review and change the publication settings.

5. Click the Package button. The plug-in's Save As dialog box appears (see Figure P-28).

164

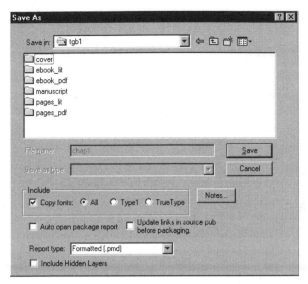

Figure P-28 The Save For Service Provider's Save As dialog box gives you options for packaging your publication.

6. Create a new folder, and double-click the folder icon.

7. Unless you know for a fact that your service provider has the fonts that your publication uses, check the Copy Fonts option and select All.

8. Click the Notes button to include a note to the printer.

9. Under Report Type, choose the file format for the report: Formatted, which creates a PageMaker file; or Text Only, which creates a text file called Report.txt. Click the Auto Open Package Report option to view the report file immediately after packaging your publication.

10. Check the Update Links In Source Pub Before Packaging option if you need to refresh linked files with the most recent versions.

11. Check the Include Hidden Layers option if you want PageMaker to package content on hidden layers.

12. Click Save.

NOTE   *If you generate a text report, it may not save in the same location as the publication package. If you don't see it, perform a search on your computer for Report.txt.*

Reverting to a Saved Publication

To revert to the most recently saved version of the publication, choose File→Revert.

Raster Graphics; see Bitmap Graphics

Reader's Spreads; see Proofs

Rectangle Tool

Use the Rectangle tool from the Toolbox to draw rectangles and squares (see Figure R-1).

Figure R-1   The Rectangle tool lets you draw rectangles and squares.

Rectangles and Squares

To draw a rectangle or square, follow these steps:

1. Select the Rectangle tool from the Toolbox. The mouse pointer becomes a crosshairs.

2. Position the crosshairs where you'd like to start drawing, hold down the mouse button, and drag. You can adjust the size and shape of the rectangle as you go (see Figure R-2). Holding down Shift while you draw changes the rectangle into a square.

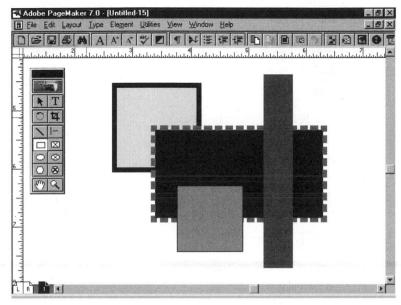

Figure R-2   The Rectangle tool drew these rectangles and squares.

3. Release the mouse button.

To round the corners of the shape, choose Element→Rounded Corners. The Rounded Corners dialog box appears. Select one of the rounding styles and click OK.

Reflecting Objects

Reflecting changes an object into its mirror image. To reflect an object, follow these steps:

1. Grab the Pointer tool from the Toolbox and select the object that you want to reflect.

2. Locate the Control palette. If you don't see it, choose Window→Show Control Palette.

3. Click the horizontal-reflect or vertical-reflect icon on the Control palette (see Figure R-3).

Figure R-3   Clicking the horizontal-reflect or vertical-reflect icon on the Control palette causes an object to become its mirror image.

TIP   *You can create backwards type by reflecting a text object.*

Replacing Text; see Finding and Changing Text

Resizing Objects

To resize an object, follow these steps:

1. With the Pointer tool from the Toolbox, select the object that you want to resize.

2. Drag a handle. Holding down Shift constrains the proportions of the object.

For more precise resizing, you can also use the Control palette.

Reverting; see Publications

RGB

RGB stands for red, green, and blue. The RGB color model is a common way to define on-screen colors, particularly for computer applications. You can create colors in PageMaker using this model.

Rotating Objects

To rotate an object, follow these steps:

1. Using the Pointer tool, select the object that you want to rotate.

2. Pick the Rotating tool from the Toolbox. The mouse pointer becomes a starburst.

3. Choose a pivot point, or the point around which you want to rotate the object. The pivot point can be inside or outside the object. Position the starburst at the pivot point, and hold down the mouse button.

4. Drag the mouse. The object rotates around the pivot point (see Figure R-4). Holding down Shift constrains the rotation to multiples of 45 degrees.

Figure R-4   The Rotating tool rotated this object.

Rotating Tool

Use the Rotating tool from the Toolbox to rotate the position of an object (see Figure R-5).

Figure R-5   The Rotating tool lets you rotate objects.

Ruler Guides

Ruler guides are horizontal or vertical straightedges that you can use to align objects. They appear in PageMaker as light blue lines, and they don't print in your final publication (see Figure R-6). To create a ruler guide, click and hold down the mouse button in the horizontal or vertical ruler, and drag a ruler guide into your publication. To remove a guide, drag it back into the ruler. To remove all ruler guides simultaneously, choose View→Clear Ruler Guides.

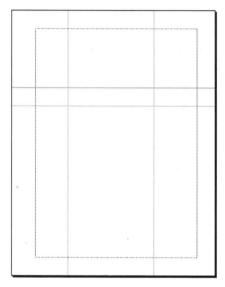

Figure R-6   These are ruler guides.

TIP   *For better design consistency, add ruler guides to master pages instead of individual publication pages.*

SEE ALSO *Guides, Layout Grids*

Rulers

The rulers in PageMaker run across the top and down the left side of the publication window. Notice that, as you move the mouse, cursors on the rulers pinpoint your exact location on the page. You can change the units of measurement for the rulers under File→Preferences→General, and you can hide the rulers under View→Hide Rulers. To force objects to align to the tick marks on the ruler, choose View→Snap To Rulers.

Rules

Rules are horizontal lines between paragraphs. Use the Paragraph Rules dialog box to apply a rule to a paragraph (see Figure R-7).

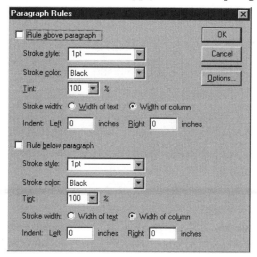

Figure R-7   Lay down the rules literally with the Paragraph Rules dialog box.

Check the Rule Above Paragraph option to add a rule above the paragraph, and set options for the style and size of the rule. Check the Rule Below Paragraph option to add a rule under the paragraph.

To modify the position of the rule, click the Options button. In the Paragraph Rule Options dialog box, type values into the Top and Bottom fields to specify the rule's position above the top baseline or below the bottom baseline. To ensure that your rules don't throw off the spacing of multicolumn text, check the Align Next Paragraph To Grid option and type the leading of the text in the Grid Size field. Since the leading value isn't likely to be a whole number, don't worry about finding the value in the list. Click OK to return to the Paragraph Rules dialog box.

To apply a rule to a paragraph, follow these steps:

1. Grab the Text tool from the Toolbox. Click inside the paragraph to which you want to apply a rule, or highlight a number of paragraphs.

2. Choose Type→Paragraph. The Paragraph Specifications dialog box appears.

3. Click the Rules button. This calls the Paragraph Rules dialog box.

4. Set the rule options, and click OK. The Paragraph Rules dialog box closes.

171

5. Click OK.

Setting rules is a paragraph-level attribute that you can define as part of a paragraph style.

SEE ALSO *Paragraph Styles*

Running Headers and Footers

To create a running header or footer that stays the same from page to page, follow these steps:

1. Turn to a master page.

2. Create a new text object, and type the header or footer.

3. Position the text object. When you turn to a publication page that refers to the master, you find the header or footer in place.

To create a running header or footer whose content depends on the page, follow these steps:

1. Using the Pointer tool from the Toolbox, select a text block that contains the story from which you want to pull the header or footer.

2. Choose Utilities→Plug-Ins→Running Headers & Footers. The Running Headers & Footers dialog box appears (see Figure R-8).

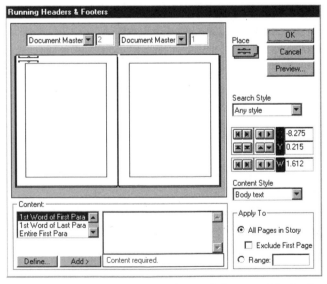

Figure R-8   Set running headers and footers with the Running Headers & Footers dialog box.

3. The thumbnails show the layout guides of the selected pages. To change the layout guides, choose different pages from the drop-down lists above the thumbnails.

4. Click the Place icon. A placeholder appears on one of the thumbnails. Drag the placeholder to position it, or use the nudge buttons next to the X and Y fields. To change the width of the placeholder, drag a handle, or use the nudge buttons next to the W field. You can also enter values directly into these fields. Press Enter to apply the new values.

5. In the Search Style list, choose the paragraph style of the text from which you want to pull the running header or footer. For instance, if you want a running header to pull from the headlines of the page, choose Headline in the Search Style list.

6. In the Content Style list, choose the paragraph style for the running header or footer.

7. Under Apply To, specify the pages on which the running header or footer should appear. Separate pages in a range with hyphens and commas, like this: 1, 3, 4-6, 8, 11-.

Skewing Objects

Skewing occurs when an object tilts to the right or left. To skew an object, follow these steps:

1. Select the object with the Pointer tool from the Toolbox.

2. Locate the Control palette. If you don't see it, choose Window→Show Control Palette.

3. Type a value in the field next to the skew icon (see Figure S-1). A negative value causes skewing to the left. A positive value causes skewing to the right. You can also use the arrow buttons to nudge the skewing value in either direction.

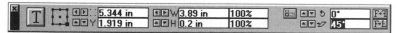

Figure S-1   Use the Control palette to skew objects.

4. Click the Apply button on the Control palette.

Source Profile

A source profile is the embedded CMS information in a graphics file. If you use color management, PageMaker can attach source profiles to your images. To do so, select the image with the Pointer tool and choose Element→Image→CMS Source.

Special Characters

Using key combinations, you can enter nonstandard characters into text objects. The following table lists some common special characters and the keys that you press to insert them:

CHARACTER	WINDOWS KEYS	MAC OS KEYS
Copyright (©)	Alt+G	Option+G
Ellipsis (…)	Hold down Alt and pressOption+;	0, 1, 3, 3 on the numeric keypad
Paragraph (¶)	Alt+7	Option+7
Registered trademark (®)	Alt+R	Option+R
Section (§)	Alt+6	Option+6
Trademark (™)	Hold down Alt and press Option+2	0, 1, 5, 3 on the numeric keypad
Single opening quote (')	Alt+[	Option+]
Single closing quote (')	Alt+]	Option+Shift+]
Double opening quote (")	Alt+Shift+[	Option+[
Double closing quote (")	Alt+Shift+]	Option+Shift+[

In addition, Windows users can enter any character, standard or non-standard, by holding down Alt and typing out 0 plus the ASCII code of the character. For instance, to type a capital A, which is almost always ASCII code 65, you could hold down Alt and press 0, 0, 6, 5. To type an upside-down question mark (¿), which is ASCII code 191 in most fonts, hold down Alt and press 0, 1, 9, 1.

For a comprehensive table of special characters, choose Help→Help Topics and click Special Characters in the contents list. To see the table, you may have to click the right-arrow graphic in the help document that loads.

SEE ALSO *Dashes, Fixed-Width Spacing*

Spelling

PageMaker can check the spelling of the text in your publication. To check spelling, follow these steps:

1. Select a text object with the Pointer tool, or, with the Text tool, highlight the text that you want to spell-check.

2. Choose Edit→Story to enter the Story Editor.

3. Choose Utilities→Spelling. The Spelling dialog box appears (see Figure S-2).

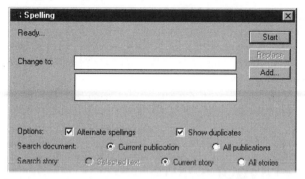

Figure S-2   Check spelling with the Spelling dialog box.

4. Under Options, check the Alternate Spellings option if you want PageMaker to suggest alternatives for misspelled words. Check the Show Duplicates option if you want PageMaker to point out instances where the same word appears twice or more in a row.

5. Under Search Document, choose whether to search the current publication or all open publications.

6. Under Search Story, choose to search the selected text, the current story, or all the stories in the publication.

7. Click Start. The spell check begins. When PageMaker comes to a word that it thinks you misspelled, it displays the word in the Change To field. If you checked the Alternate Spellings option in Step 3, you can select one of the alternatives in the text box underneath the word and click Replace. To add the word to your user dictionary, click Add. To move on, click Ignore.

8. When the spell check finishes, close the Spelling dialog box by clicking the X in the upper right corner.

Spot Colors

Spot color is different from process color in that the commercial printer applies premixed ink to a separate plate to print the color. Spot color reproduces better than standard process color, but it can become expensive. Use spot color to enhance monochrome or mostly monochrome publications, or call for spot color when design elements need to reproduce exactly in otherwise process-colored jobs.

Squares; see Rectangles and Squares

Stacking Order

Every layer in PageMaker has a stacking order that determines which objects sit in front of which other objects on the layer. You can change an object's position in the stacking order with the Arrange command in the Element menu.

SEE ALSO *Arranging Objects*

Stars; see Polygons and Stars

Story

A story in PageMaker is a complete piece of text. A single story can thread through multiple text objects.

Story Editor

The Story Editor is a word-processor-style environment that you can use to edit text (see Figure S-3). The Story Editor doesn't display images or most formatting and page-layout options. Instead, it allows you to focus solely on the text, and it gives you Find, Change, and Spelling commands that you don't get in the layout view. Highlight and change text in the Story Editor just as you would in a text object. When you finish, switch back to layout view to adjust the position of the story on the page.

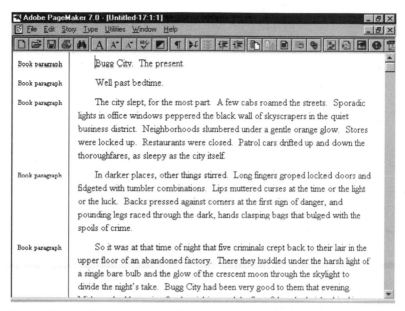

Figure. S-3   Use the Story Editor to work with text.

Choose Edit ▸ Edit Story to open the Story Editor. By default, the Story Editor displays the names of paragraph styles in the left margin. You can turn off this option by removing the check mark next to Display Style Names in the Story menu. View invisible characters like spaces and paragraph marks in the Story Editor by placing a check mark next to the Show ¶ option. To return to the layout view, choose Edit→Edit Layout.

NOTE   *You can have multiple Story Editor windows open at the same time. Choose Window→Tile or Window→Cascade to manage multiple windows.*

Opening a Story

To open a story in the Story Editor from the layout view, select the story with the Pointer tool and choose Edit→Edit Story.

Creating a New Story

To create a new story in the Story Editor, choose Story→New Story. Type the new story in the Story Editor. When you finish, select Edit→Edit Layout to return to the layout view. Position the mouse pointer where you want to place the new story, and click the mouse button.

TIP   *You can place the new story inside an empty frame. If you plan to do this, first create the frame in the layout. Then, switch to the Story Editor to write the story. When you return to the layout view, click inside the frame.*

Placing a Story

Choose File→Place to import a text file into the Story Editor. Windows users can click the Place icon on the Toolbar.

Placing an Inline Graphic

To place an inline graphic when you're in the Story Editor, select File→Place and navigate to the image file in the Import To Story Editor dialog box. Double-click the icon to place the image. The Story Editor inserts a placeholder character to represent the graphic. To see the graphic, return to the layout view.

Changing the Paragraph Style

To change the style of a paragraph in the Story Editor, click anywhere in the paragraph to select it. Then, in the Styles palette, click the name of the style you want to apply. The text may change slightly, but remember that the Story Editor doesn't display most formatting. To see the actual formatting, switch back to the layout view.

Changing Story Editor Preferences

In the Story Editor preferences, you can change the font and the size of the text, and you can choose to display paragraph style names and invisible characters by default. To change preferences for the Story Editor, choose File→Preferences→General. Click the More button on the Preferences dialog box, and look under Story Editor in the More Preferences dialog box.

SEE ALSO *Finding and Changing Text, Spelling*

Stroke

The stroke of an object is its outline or contour. An object's stroke can have a color and style different from the object's fill. To apply a stroke to an object, select the object with the Pointer tool and choose Element→Fill and Stroke. Then, in the Fill And Stroke dialog box, pick a style, color, and tint for the fill. Check the Overprint option if you want the stroke to print on top of colors in the background instead of knocking them out. Check the Transparent Background option if you want gaps in the stroke style to be transparent. Check the Reverse option to create a stroke with the same color as the paper. To create or edit a stroke quickly, choose Element→Stroke.

NOTE   *Text blocks and independent graphics don't take the stroke attribute. Use text frames instead of text blocks if you want to apply a stroke to a text object, and choose Utilities→Keyline to add an outline to an independent graphic.*

Table of Contents

PageMaker makes it easy for you to create a table of contents for your publication. The first step is to identify the items that you want to appear in the table of contents, which are usually the headings and subheadings of your publication. Add these items to the table of contents in one of three ways:

- Using the Text tool, click inside the heading or subheading that you want to include. Choose Type→Paragraph, and check the Include In Table Of Contents option on the Paragraph Specifications dialog box. Repeat this step for every item in your publication.

- Define or edit the paragraph style that you use for your headings and subheadings. Click the Para button in the Style Options dialog box, and check the Include In Table Of Contents option in the Paragraph Specifications dialog box. Every headline or subhead that refers to this style automatically becomes part of the table of contents. If this doesn't sell you on paragraph styles, nothing will!

- Use the default PageMaker paragraph styles of Headline, Subhead 1, and Subhead 2 for your headings and subheadings. PageMaker predefines these styles to appear in the table of contents.

Once you identify the table of contents entries, choose Utilities→Create TOC. The Create Table Of Contents dialog box appears (see Figure T-1).

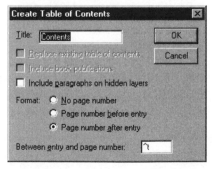

Figure T-1   The Create Table Of Contents dialog box makes it easy to generate a table of contents.

Type a title for the table of contents (TOC) in the appropriate field, and choose from the following options:

- Check the Replace Existing Table Of Contents option to overwrite the current TOC with a new one.

179

- If your publication has a book list, check the Include Book Publications option to create a TOC for the entire book. Please note that you must copy the book list to every publication in the book for this option to work.

- Check the Include Paragraphs On Hidden Layers option to search text objects on hidden layers for TOC entries.

- Under Format, specify how you want the entries to appear.

- Type a separator string in the Between Entry And Page Number field. The default is the tab character, or ^t. You can type up to seven characters for the separator string.

Click the OK button to generate the table of contents. Then, add a new page to your publication, or turn to the page where you want the table of contents to appear. Position the mouse pointer and click to place your table of contents as a new story. If your TOC is longer than a page, you may want to turn on the Autoflow feature in the Layout menu before you place the TOC. Otherwise, flow the story manually.

After you place the table of contents, you can modify its appearance by editing the TOC styles in the Styles palette. Make spot changes to the entries with the Text tool.

Be aware that PageMaker doesn't automatically update the table of contents after you place it. If you make significant changes to your publication, you may throw off the TOC. For this reason, generate the table of contents after you finalize your work. If you need to re-create the TOC, rerun the utility and check the Replace Existing Table Of Contents option.

Tables

Use Adobe Table 3.0 to create tables for your PageMaker publication (see Figure T-2). Adobe Table is a standalone application that comes on the PageMaker 7.0 Application CD. You can find this program in the PageMaker 7.0 application folder. Windows users can launch Adobe Table under Start→Programs→Adobe→PageMaker 7.0.

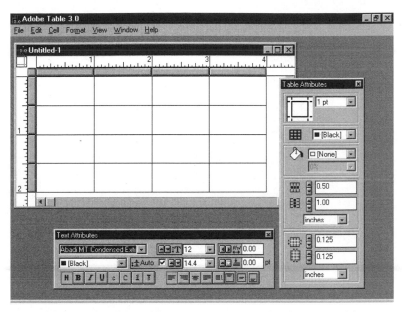

Figure T-2   Use Adobe Table 3.0 to create tables for your publication.

Adobe Table defines a table as a matrix of horizontal rows and vertical columns. The intersection of a row and a column is a cell, which holds content.

Creating a Table

To create a table in Adobe Table, choose File→New from the Adobe Table menu and choose the physical dimensions of the table as well as the number of rows and columns. You can change these properties later, so don't worry about being exact.

To enter content, click in a cell with the mouse pointer and type. Set the font, alignment, and style of the text with the Text Attributes palette. Set the background color and border style of the cell with the Table Attributes palette. You can set the attributes for an entire row or column by clicking the button at the top of the row or to the left of the column. This selects all the cells in the row or column, and any changes you make to the Text or Table Attributes palette apply to all the selected cells.

To add a row or column to the table, look under the Cell menu for Insert Row Above, Insert Row Below, Insert Column Before, and Insert Column After commands. To delete a row or column, select the row or column and choose Cell→Delete Row or Cell→Delete Column.

To change the size of the rows or columns, drag the black space between the row and column buttons. Use the vertical and horizontal rulers as a guide to laying out the table.

Use File→Save and File→Save As commands to save your work.

Exporting a Table from Adobe Table

You must export your table to use it in a PageMaker publication. Adobe Table gives you two options for exporting:

- Text format, which exports the text of the table but doesn't export color, font, text style, or alignment. If you export in this format, you can edit the text in PageMaker.

- Graphic format, which saves the entire table as an EPS file. If you export in this format, you can't edit the content of the table.

To export a table, choose File→Export→Text or File→Export→Graphic.

Importing a Table into PageMaker

Import the table like any other text or graphics file: by using the Place command.

Tabs

Use tabs to align columns of data inside text objects. The Indents/Tabs ruler lets you define the tab stops of a paragraph (see Figure T-3).

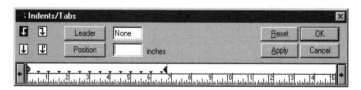

Figure T-3   Define tabs with the Indents/Tabs ruler.

To open the Indents/Tabs ruler, click a paragraph with the Text tool and choose Type→Indents/Tabs, or edit a paragraph style and click the Tabs button. The small inverted triangles in the white space above the ruler indicate the default tab stops of the paragraph.

To create a new tab stop in the selected paragraph or paragraph style, first click the arrow icon of the tab you want to create. Find the arrow icons in the upper left corner of the Indents/Tabs ruler. In clockwise order, the icons represent left-aligned, right-aligned, decimal-aligned, and centered tabs. Then, position the mouse pointer on the ruler at the spot where you want to place the tab, and click. The tab marker appears in the white space above the ruler, and any default tab stops to the left of the icon disappear.

If you want to add a leader, or a string of characters, between your tab and the next tab stop, click the Leader button, and choose a leader style from the list. To create your own leader style, choose Custom, and then type the leader in the field.

Click the Position button to open a menu with additional tab commands:

- Type a value in the Position field, and choose Add Tab to place a tab stop at that position.

- Click a tab marker, and choose Delete Tab to remove it.

- Click a tab marker, type a new value in the Position field, and choose Move Tab to move the marker to the new position.

- Click a tab marker, type a value in the Position field, and choose Repeat Tab to place new tab stops at whatever interval you specify in the Position field.

You can drag a tab to a new position along the ruler by clicking the tab marker, holding down the mouse button, and moving the mouse. As you drag the marker to the left, the default tab stops reappear. As you drag it to the right, the defaults disappear. Change the tab stop by clicking the marker and choosing a new arrow icon or modifying the leader style.

To set your tabs, click the Apply button. To remove your tabs and reset the defaults, click Reset. Click OK to close the Indents/Tabs ruler.

SEE ALSO *Hanging Indents, Indents*

Targeting Bitmap Graphics; see Graphics

Templates

A template is a publication with predefined objects. PageMaker provides a library of publication templates in the Template palette (see Figure T-4). Use these to create a design for your publication quickly. You can also create your own templates and add them to the Template palette. If you don't see the Template palette on screen, choose Window→Plug-In Palettes→Show Template Palette.

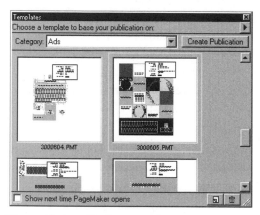

Figure T-4   Design a publication in record time by borrowing from the Template palette.

Browse the templates by choosing a category from the Category list. Your choices appear in the main window of the palette as thumbnails. To open a template as a new publication, double-click the thumbnail. The objects in the template work just like the objects in a normal publication. You can move them, edit them, add text to them, or customize them however you like.

Edit the categories or reorganize the templates with the commands on the Template palette menu, which opens when you click the triangle icon in the upper right of the palette (see Figure T-5). You can reorganize multiple templates at once by holding down Shift as you select the thumbnails. Change the size of the thumbnails in the palette by choosing Palette Options from the Template palette menu.

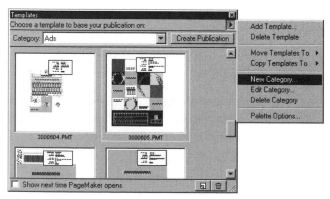

Figure T-5   Open the Template palette menu by clicking the triangle icon.

Creating a Template

To create your own PageMaker template, follow these steps:

1. Open the publication that you want to use as a template.
2. Choose File→Save As, and select Template from the Save As Type list on the Save Publication dialog box. Save the template in a convenient location on your hard drive. You may want to keep all your templates in a single folder.
3. From the Category list on the Template palette, select the category to which you want to add the template.
4. Click the new-page icon at the bottom of the Template palette. The new-page icon is next to the trashcan icon. This opens the Add A Template dialog box (see Figure T-6).

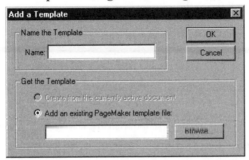

Figure T-6   Create your own template with the Add A Template dialog box.

5. Type a name for the template, and click OK. A thumbnail of your template appears in the Template palette.
6. To change your template's category, select Move Templates To from the Template palette menu.

Text

As you work with text, keep in mind that PageMaker distinguishes between character-level edits and paragraph-level edits. If you make a paragraph-level edit, like setting alignment, all the text in the paragraph acquires the change.

Selecting Text

Use the Text tool from the Toolbox to select text. To select an individual character or a group of characters, highlight the characters by holding down the mouse button and dragging the mouse. To select a single paragraph, click anywhere in the paragraph. To select multiple paragraphs, highlight them. To select all the text in a story, click anywhere in the story and choose Edit→Select All. This command selects text in other text objects if the story threads. If you want to edit the text in only a single threaded text object, highlight the text manually.

Cutting, Copying, and Pasting Text

To cut or copy text, highlight the text and choose Edit→Cut or Edit→Copy. To paste a single copy of the text, choose Edit→Paste. To paste multiple copies of the text, choose Edit→Paste Multiple.

Aligning Text

To align text, select the text and choose Type→Alignment. There are five alignment options: left, center, right, justify, and force justify. Text alignment is a paragraph-level attribute.

Formatting Text

The Control palette gives you ten text-formatting options (see Figure T-7). From left to right, they are:

- Normal
- Bold
- Italic
- Underline, which adds a thin line underneath the body of the character
- Reverse, which colors the character the same as the paper
- Strikethrough, which adds a thin line through the character
- Caps/Small Caps, which displays lowercase letters as smaller versions of the capital letter
- All Caps, which displays lowercase letters as full-size capital letters
- Superscript, which makes the character smaller and positions it above the baseline
- Subscript, which makes the character smaller and positions it below the baseline

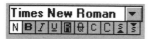

Figure T-7   Format text with the Control palette.

In many cases, you can choose multiple formats for a single piece of text. For instance, text can be bold and italic. A few of the formats are mutually exclusive, meaning that selecting one automatically deselects the other. For example, a character can't be a superscript and a subscript simultaneously, at least not in this dimension.

To format text as you type, click the appropriate formatting icon on the Control palette. To format existing text, highlight it, and then click the icon on the Control palette. Text formatting is a character-level attribute.

NOTE   *Watch out for underlines and strikethroughs if you use the Caps/ Small Caps, Superscript, or Subscript formats. You may find that underlines and strikethroughs don't line up correctly.*

Breaking Lines of Type

Pressing Enter breaks the line of type at the position of the cursor, but it also creates a new paragraph. To insert a line break without creating a new paragraph, press Shift+Enter.

If you don't want a line to break where it does, highlight the words before and after the break and choose Type→Character. The Character Specifications dialog box appears. Choose No Break from the Line Break list and click OK.

Controlling Column and Page Breaks

To control column and page breaks, select a paragraph and choose Type→Paragraph. The Paragraph Specifications dialog box appears. Select from the following options:

- Check the Keep Lines Together option if you don't want the paragraph to break at a column or page.
- Check the Keep With Next x Lines option, and specify a value for x, to keep the last line of the current paragraph with the next x lines of the following paragraph. The value of x may be zero, one, two, or three.
- Check the Column Break Before option to force the paragraph to move to the top of the next column.
- Check the Page Break Before option to force the paragraph to move to the top of the next page.
- A widow is the beginning of a paragraph when it appears at the bottom of a column or page. To prevent widows, check Widow Control, and specify the number of lines that must appear before the column or paragraph breaks. The maximum value is three.
- An orphan is the tail end of a paragraph when it appears at the top of a column or page. To prevent orphans, check Orphan Control, and specify the number of lines that must appear at the top of the column or page. The maximum value is three.

PageMaker may not always be able to comply with all your column-break and page-break requests, particularly if you use several at once.

187

By opening the Preferences dialog box with File→Preferences →General and checking the Show "Keeps" Violations option, you can instruct PageMaker to highlight the lines that it isn't able to manage.

SEE ALSO   *Finding and Changing Text, Spelling, Text Objects, Text Tool, Threading Stories, Type Size, Wrapping Text Around an Object*

Text Objects

There are two kinds of text objects in PageMaker: the text block and the text frame. Each has its strengths. Text blocks work best with book- and newspaper-style layouts, where the running text is the star of the show. Text frames are better for magazines and brochures, which rely more heavily on dynamic composition.

Text Blocks

Text blocks have the following properties:

- Text blocks are always rectangular in shape.
- Text blocks have no stroke and fill attributes.
- Text blocks change size as you add or remove text. The width of a text block remains constant, but its height depends on the amount of text it contains.
- Using threaded text blocks, you can flow a story automatically from column to column or page to page.
- Text blocks work with all text-based plug-ins, such as Add Cont'd Line and Balance Columns.

To create a text block that starts at the left margin of the column or page and ends at the right margin, follow these steps:

1. Select the Text tool from the Toolbox. The mouse pointer becomes an I-beam.

2. Move the mouse pointer inside the page margins. Choose the vertical position of the text block, and click.

3. A flashing cursor appears on the left margin of the column or page. Begin typing. When you reach the right margin, the text automatically wraps to the next line (see Figure T-8).

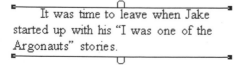

Figure T-8   This text appears in a text block.

To create a text block with borders different from the column or page margins, follow these steps:

1. Select the Text tool from the Toolbox. The mouse pointer becomes an I-beam.

2. Position the mouse pointer where you want the text block to begin, hold down the mouse button, and drag. Release the mouse button when the text box reaches the desired size.

3. A flashing cursor appears in the upper left corner of the text block. Begin typing. The text automatically wraps to the next line when you reach the right side of the text block.

Text Frames

Text frames have the following properties:

- Text frames can be any shape.
- Text frames have stroke and fill attributes.
- Text frames don't change size as you add or remove text. If you run out of room, you must resize the frame or thread the text.
- A story can flow from column to column or page to page using threaded text frames, but you must thread each frame manually.
- Text frames don't always work with text-based plug-ins.

To create a text frame, follow these steps:

1. Pick the frame tool of your choice—Rectangle, Ellipse, or Polygon—from the Toolbox. The mouse pointer becomes a crosshairs.

2. Position the mouse pointer where you want the text frame to begin, and draw the frame.

3. Select the Text tool from the Toolbox. The mouse pointer becomes an I-beam.

4. Position the mouse pointer inside the frame and click.

5. A flashing cursor appears. Begin typing. The text automatically wraps to the next line when you reach the right side of the frame. If you add more text than the frame can hold, PageMaker beeps at you. You must resize the current text frame or thread the text into another frame (see Figure T-9).

Ray wanted real life to be
more like a comic book, provided
that his thoughts wouldn't appear
in balloons.

Figure T-9   This text appears in a text frame.

Text Size; see Type Size

Text Tool

Use the Text tool from the Toolbox to create text blocks and edit text in your publication (see Figure T-10).

Figure T-10   The Text tool lets you create text blocks and edit text.

Threading Stories

When a story doesn't fit into a single text object, you can thread the story into other text objects. You can tell that a text object has more text than it can hold when the bottom windowshade handle turns red. The procedure for threading the story changes slightly, depending on the type of text object that contains the thread. The characteristics of the thread itself also change. While PageMaker can add threaded text blocks automatically with the Autoflow feature, you must thread text frames manually. However, text frames give you better control over the flow of the thread.

Threading Text Blocks

To thread a story between text blocks, follow these steps:

190

1. With the Pointer tool, select the overfilled text block.

2. Click the red windowshade handle. The mouse pointer becomes the loaded-text icon.

3. Position the mouse pointer where you want to continue the story, and click. PageMaker creates a text block to fill the rest of the page. You may also hold down the mouse button and drag to define the size of the new text block. Release the mouse button, and PageMaker creates the new text block.

TIP   *To add as many threaded text blocks as you need to place the entire story, put a check mark next to the Autoflow option in the Layout menu.*

Threading Text Frames

To thread a story between text frames, follow these steps:

1. Using one of the frame tools, draw a new frame in your publication.

2. With the Pointer tool, select the overfilled text frame.

3. Click the red windowshade handle. The mouse pointer becomes the threading icon.

4. Position the mouse pointer in the empty frame that you drew in Step 1, and click.

Breaking the Thread in a Text Frame

In a text frame, to break the thread of the story, follow these steps:

1. Using the Pointer tool, select the text frame. Note the top and bottom windowshade handles. If the bottom windowshade contains a plus sign, it means that the story threads to another frame. If the top windowshade contains a plus sign, it means that the frame receives threaded text from another frame.

2. Windows users should press Ctrl+Shift and click the top or bottom plus sign. Mac OS users should press Command+Shift and click the top or bottom plus sign. The thread breaks at the place you click.

Redirecting the Thread Among Text Frames

To redirect the thread of a story among text frames, follow these steps:

1. Using the Pointer tool, select the text frame whose text you want to redirect.

2. Break the thread.

3. Select the frame to which you want to redirect the story. If this frame contains a plus sign in the top windowshade handle, break the thread.

191

4. Now, reselect the frame from Step 1 and click the red windowshade handle. The mouse pointer becomes the link icon. Position the mouse pointer in the frame from Step 3, and click. The story rethreads.

Unthreading a Text Frame

To remove a text frame from the thread, select the text frame with the Pointer tool and choose Element→Frame→Remove From Threads.

Deleting a Threaded Text Object

To delete a threaded text object, select the text object with the Pointer tool and choose Edit→Clear. If you delete a text block, you also delete the text that it contains. Unless you want to remove the text, you should shrink the text block so that it contains no text before you delete it. If you delete a text frame, the text continues to the next frame in the thread—the text doesn't disappear with the frame.

Tight Lines

Tight lines are lines of type with too little space between the words (see Figure T-11). The text seems packed together, and the words may be difficult to read. PageMaker can highlight the tight lines in your publication if you select File→Preferences→General and check the Show Loose/Tight Lines option.

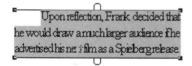

Figure T-11   These lines are tight.

SEE ALSO *Loose Lines*

Tints

A tint is a lighter shade of a color in your publication. In PageMaker, there are two kinds of tints: color-level tints, or colors that always appear as tints; and object-level tints, or colors that appear as tints in specific objects only.

To create a color-level tint, click the new-page icon on the Colors palette to open the Color Options dialog box. Select Tint from the Type menu. Choose the base color, and drag the slider to create the desired shade. Type a name for the tint and click OK.

To create an object-level tint, select the object with the Pointer tool. Locate the Colors palette, and choose a new value from the Tint list at the top of the palette.

TIP   *In a world where adding spot colors to your publication can make your printing costs soar, recycling existing spot colors as tints can enhance your publication's palette while saving you money. For instance, if your publication includes a spot-color blue, you have the full range of blue tints to use as spot colors at no additional cost.*

Toolbar

PageMaker 7.0 for Windows includes a Toolbar along the top of the screen (see Figure T-12). The Toolbar includes icons for common PageMaker commands like File→Place, Type→Character, and View→Zoom In.

Figure T-12   If you're a Windows user, the Toolbar gives you icons for common PageMaker commands.

To turn the Toolbar into a floating palette, drag it into the publication. You can also dock the Toolbar to the left, right, and bottom of the screen by dragging it to the left, right, or bottom. To make the Toolbar invisible or visible again, choose Utilities→Plug-Ins→Show/Hide ToolBar.

NOTE   *If you have Photoshop, PageMaker puts a familiar icon on the Toolbar. Click this icon to launch Photoshop.*

Toolbox

The Toolbox is the tall, narrow floating window that contains the fourteen tool icons (see Figure T-13). To hide the Toolbox, choose Window→Hide Tools. To show the Toolbox after hiding it, choose Window→Show Tools.

Figure T-13   The Toolbox contains the set of tools.

Tracking

Tracking is the amount of space between words and characters in a line of type. It affects the visual density of the page. Tight tracking makes the page feel heavier, while loose tracking makes it feel lighter. The fonts on your computer have built-in tracking values, but you can override these with PageMaker's Expert Tracking command. To apply tracking to a line of type, follow these steps:

1. Use the Text tool to highlight the text you want to track.

2. Choose Type→Expert Tracking and select a tracking option from the menu that slides out. The Normal option represents the font's built-in tracking. PageMaker's alternatives range from Very Tight to Very Loose (see Figure T-14).

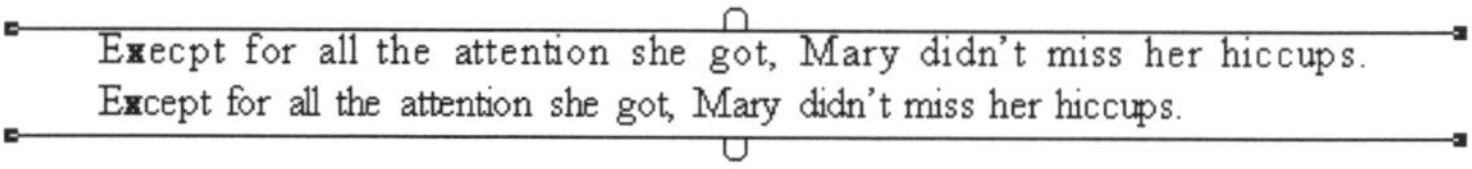

Figure T-14   This text block has two lines: one with very loose tracking, and one with very tight tracking.

Tracking is a character-level attribute that you can set as part of a paragraph style.

NOTE   *You can edit the tracks for a font with Type→Expert Tracking→Edit Tracks. However, doing so changes the tracks for the font every time you use it in PageMaker.*

SEE ALSO   *Paragraph Styles*

Trapping

PageMaker uses trapping in separation printing to ensure that colors appear in the proper place on the page. Trapping in PageMaker involves overprinting, or laying a trap color directly on top of background colors. To review the trapping options for your publication, choose File→Preferences→Trapping (see Figure T-15).

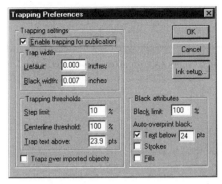

Figure T-15   Fine-tune trapping options with the Trapping Preferences dialog box, but check with your service provider first.

To turn on trapping, check the Enable Trapping For Publication option. Consult with your commercial printer, and then adjust the other trapping options if necessary.

NOTE   *PageMaker doesn't trap placed graphics. You can trap images independently before placing them with applications like Photoshop and Illustrator.*

Type Size

PageMaker measures type size in points. To adjust the point size of text in your publication, follow these steps:

1. Use the Text tool to select the text whose size you want to change.

2. Choose Type→Size, and select a standard point size from the list that slides out. If you want to use a nonstandard size, select the Other option and type the point value in the Other Point Size dialog box. You can specify type in tenth-point increments.

Type size is a character-level attribute that you can define as part of a paragraph style.

SEE ALSO *Paragraph Styles*

Type Style

Type style is another term for text formatting: bold, italic, underline, strikethrough, and so on.

SEE ALSO *Text*

Undo

PageMaker offers a de facto Undo command in the Edit menu. When the command works, which isn't often, it can remove the most recent change to your publication. The following table lists common changes and whether PageMaker lets you undo them:

CHANGE	UNDOABLE?
Adding ruler guides	Yes
Adjusting columns	Yes
Adjusting margins	Yes
Aligning and distributing objects	No
Applying fills	No
Applying master pages	Yes
Applying paragraph styles	No
Applying strokes	No
Arranging objects	No
Autoflowing text	Yes
Drawing objects	No
Editing character-level attributes	No
Editing paragraph-level attributes	No
Grouping objects	Yes
Inserting pages	No
Moving guides	Yes
Moving objects	Yes
Pasting objects	No
Pasting text	Yes
Placing objects	No
Removing pages	No
Resizing objects	Yes
Typing text	Yes
Ungrouping objects	Yes

CHANGE	UNDOABLE?
Using plug-ins	No
Wrapping text	No

You may want to do frequent mini-saves of your work instead, and restore your publication to the mini-saved state when the need arises.

SEE ALSO *Mini-Save*

URL Destination

A URL destination is a hyperlink target on the Web. Use the Hyperlinks palette to define or import URL destinations.

User Dictionaries

A user dictionary is a list of words that supplements a PageMaker language dictionary. The user dictionary contains words that the default language dictionary doesn't, such as technical terms and proper names. You can add words to the user dictionary for your language as you check spelling or set up hyphenation, or you can use the standalone Dictionary Editor application (see Figure U-1). Windows users can find this program under Start→Programs→Adobe→PageMaker 7.0. Mac OS users can find it under Typography in the PageMaker application folder.

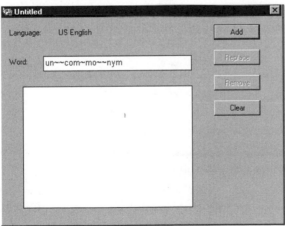

Figure U-1   The Dictionary Editor application lets you create and edit user dictionaries for PageMaker.

While the Dictionary Editor allows you to create a user dictionary from scratch, you probably want to open and modify the current user dictionary instead. This way, you won't lose words that you may have already added using PageMaker commands.

Opening the Current User Dictionary

To open the current user dictionary with the Dictionary Editor, follow these steps:

1. Launch the Dictionary Editor.

2. Choose File→Open. The Open User Dictionary dialog box appears.

3. Navigate to the current user-dictionary file for your language and double-click the icon. You can find the user dictionary in the PageMaker application folder. For example, to find the current U.S. English user dictionary, Windows users can look under c:\Program Files\Adobe\PageMaker7.0\RSRC\Linguist\PRX\USENGLSH\.

Creating a New User Dictionary

To create a new user dictionary with the Dictionary Editor, follow these steps:

1. Launch the Dictionary Editor.

2. Choose File→New. The Create User Dictionary dialog box appears.

3. Type a filename for the user dictionary, and choose the language dictionary that your user dictionary supplements. Click OK.

NOTE   *If you create a new user dictionary, you must install it after you save it for PageMaker to use it. Your new user dictionary replaces the current one.*

Editing a User Dictionary

To edit a user dictionary with the Dictionary Editor, follow these steps:

1. Launch the Dictionary Editor.

2. Open an existing user dictionary, or create a new one. The window for the user dictionary appears.

3. If you want to add or replace a word, type the new word in the Word field, indicating hyphenation break points with tildes (~). Type one tilde for best-choice break points, two tildes for average break points, and three tildes for acceptable break points. Click the Add button to add the word to the user dictionary, or highlight the word that you want to replace and click the Replace button. To erase the Word field without adding or replacing anything, click Clear.

4. To remove a word from the user dictionary, highlight it and click Remove.

5. When you finish editing the user dictionary, choose File→Save or File→Save As from the menu.

TIP   *To apply a hyphenation algorithm to the word, type it normally, without any tildes. Then, choose Edit→Hyphenate. You may want to double-check that the word breaks correctly, since the algorithm can make poor choices.*

Importing a Word List

To import a list of words for the user dictionary, follow these steps:

1. Prepare the word list in a text editor. Type the entries the way that you want them to appear in the user dictionary, adding tildes for hyphenation break points if you desire. Insert a carriage return after each word, and save the file in plain-text format.

2. Launch the Dictionary Editor.

3. Open an existing user dictionary, or create a new one. The window for the user dictionary appears.

4. Choose File→Import. The Import From Text File dialog box appears.

5. If you want PageMaker to apply the hyphenation algorithm to the words in the list, check the Hyphenate On Import Using Algorithm option. If you want PageMaker to replace words from the list that already appear in the user dictionary, check the Import Words Already In Dictionary option.

6. Navigate to the text file that contains the word list, and double-click the icon.

Exporting a Word List

To save your user dictionary as a word list in plain-text format, choose File→Export.

Installing a User Dictionary

You can install only one user dictionary at a time for any given language. If you want to install a new user dictionary, thereby uninstalling the current one, choose File→Install. The Install User Dictionary dialog box appears.Confirm that you want to replace the current user dictionary, and click the Install button.

To reinstall a previously uninstalled user dictionary, open the old user dictionary with the File→Open command and then choose File→Install.

SEE ALSO *Language Dictionaries*

Vector Graphics

Vector graphics are computer files that describe an image in terms of shapes and outlines, not pixels. For this reason, vector graphics scale, or change size, much more reliably than bitmaps. PageMaker supports the EPS graphics format, which is vector-based. If you place an EPS image in your publication, you can resize it in PageMaker with confidence.

Web Pages; see HTML Files

Windowshade Handles

Windowshade handles appear around a frame or text block when you click it with the Pointer tool (see Figure W-1). The windowshades indicate whether the selected object links to another object and in which direction. For instance, if the top windowshade shows a plus sign, it means that the object receives the thread of a story from another object. However, if the bottom windowshade is a red inverted triangle, it means that the object has more text than it can hold. Create a new text object and thread the overflow into it.

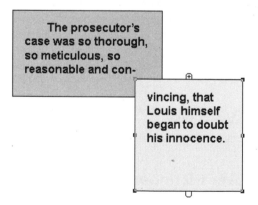

Figure W-1   Windowshade handles give threading information about a frame or text block.

NOTE   *Windowshades appear around graphics frames, too, even though graphics frames can't thread stories.*

Word Counter

Use the Word Counter plug-in to count words, characters, sentences, paragraphs, text objects, and stories. Generate statistics for the following:

- To generate statistics for the entire publication, deselect all objects by clicking on an empty area of the page with the Pointer tool.
- To generate statistics for an entire story, click anywhere inside the story with the Text tool and choose Edit→Select All.
- To generate statistics for a particular text object, select the text object with the Pointer tool. You can select multiple text objects by holding down the Shift key as you click. You can also choose Edit→Select All to select all the objects on the screen—the Word Counter ignores all nontext objects.
- To generate statistics for a portion of a text object, highlight the text with the Text tool.

Afterward, choose Utilities→Plug-Ins→Word Counter.

Work Area; see Pasteboard

Wrapping Text Around an Object

You can wrap text blocks and text frames around most of the other design elements in your publication. For instance, if your design calls for a large image in the center of the page, the surrounding text can begin to the left of the image, skip over the image itself, and continue to the right. To wrap text around an object, follow these steps:

1. Use the Pointer tool to select the object around which you want to wrap text.

2. Choose Element→Text Wrap. The Text Wrap dialog box appears.

3. Click the middle icon under Wrap Option.

4. Under Text Flow, click the icon that best illustrates the way you want the text to wrap around the object.

5. Under Standoff, supply values for the object's text-wrap boundary, or the amount of space between the text and the edge of the object. The larger the boundary, the sooner the text wraps as it approaches the object.

6. Check the Wrap Text On Same Layer Only option if you don't want the text on other layers to wrap around the object.

7. Click OK. The text-wrap boundary appears around the object as a dotted line.

8. Using the Pointer tool, drag the object, and superimpose it on the text that you want to wrap.

By default, the object's boundary is rectangular, but you can turn it into a parallelogram or a polygon. To modify the shape of an object's boundary, grab the Pointer tool from the Toolbox and select the object. Note the four black points in the corners of the boundary. These are the boundary's handles. Drag the boundary's handles, or drag the dotted lines between the handles, to change the shape. Holding down Shift while you drag constrains the adjustment to horizontal and vertical. To create a new handle, position the mouse pointer on the dotted line, click the mouse button, and release. Then, drag the new handle.

To change a parallelogram or polygon boundary back into a rectangle, select the object with the Pointer tool, choose Element→Text Wrap, and click the middle icon under Wrap Option. To change the way that text wraps around the object, pick a different icon under Text Flow. To turn off text wrap altogether, click the left icon under Wrap Option.

You can wrap text around text frames, graphics frames, drawn objects, and placed graphics. You can't wrap text around text blocks unless you first turn the text block into a group with Element→Group.

Zooming In and Out

PageMaker gives you many choose View commands for changing your view of the publication:

Choose View→Zoom In to come closer, Choose View→Zoom Out to go back, and so forth.

You can also use the Magnify tool much like the View→Zoom In and View→Zoom Out commands. Grab the Magnify tool from the Toolbox and click on an area of the Pasteboard to come closer. To go back, Windows users should click the mouse button while holding down Ctrl, and Mac OS users should click the mouse button while holding down Option. Double-click the Magnify tool to view the actual size of the publication, or double-click the Magnify tool while holding down Alt in Windows or Option in Mac OS to fit the publication in the window.